LEGENDS OF WARFARE

AVIATION

F-15 Eagle

McDonnell Douglas Strike Fighter

DAVID DOYLE

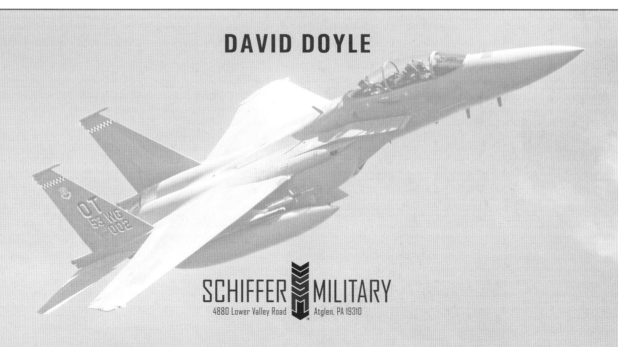

SCHIFFER MILITARY

4880 Lower Valley Road ▪ Atglen, PA 19310

Cover design by Justin Watkinson
Type set in Impact/Minion Pro/Univers LT Std

ISBN: 978-0-7643-6707-6
Printed in India

Published by Schiffer Publishing, Ltd.
4880 Lower Valley Road
Atglen, PA 19310
Phone: (610) 593-1777; Fax: (610) 593-2002
Email: Info@schifferbooks.com
Web: www.schifferbooks.com

For our complete selection of fine books on this and related subjects, please visit our website at www.schifferbooks.com. You may also write for a free catalog.

Schiffer Publishing's titles are available at special discounts for bulk purchases for sales promotions or premiums. Special editions, including personalized covers, corporate imprints, and excerpts, can be created in large quantities for special needs. For more information, contact the publisher.

We are always looking for people to write books on new and related subjects. If you have an idea for a book, please contact us at proposals@schifferbooks.com.

Acknowledgments

As with all of my projects, this book would not have been possible without the generous help of many friends. Instrumental to the completion of this book were Tom Kailbourn, Dana Bell, Chris Hughes, Scott Taylor, the staff of the Still Pictures Unit of the National Archives, and Brett Stolle at the National Museum of the United States Air Force. The Lord has blessed me with a wonderful wife, Denise, who not only scanned countless images for this and other efforts but also provides ongoing support and encouragement throughout these projects.

All photos not otherwise credited are from the US Department of Defense.

Contents

Introduction

First flying in 1972, the McDonnell Douglas F-15 Eagle has transitioned from a true air superiority fighter into an all-weather strike aircraft. Thus far, the aircraft has compiled one of the most enviable records of a post-Vietnam fighter, logging over 100 victories and no losses in air-to-air combat.

The bulk of the fighter aircraft operated by the USAF in Vietnam had been conceived during the Cold War as interceptors against nuclear-armed Soviet bombers. This strategy involved high-altitude, high-speed, air-to-air missile armament, and a long range. Utilizing these aircraft in Vietnam, with visual engagement rules, pointed to the shortcomings of the planning. Though both the F-105 and F-4 were deployed to Vietnam, neither was truly optimized for the role that it was forced into.

Further shortcomings of the then-current fighter strategy was revealed in July 1967, when the Soviets unveiled the MiG-25 Foxbat. The Foxbat was a twin-tail, twin-engine fighter aircraft capable of Mach 2.8. The US Air Force responded with renewed interest in what was then known as the F-X program. This program had begun as an effort to develop a multirole aircraft with variable-geometry wings. After briefly considering a lightweight, single-engine fighter, a concept discarded in light of the shortcomings of the F-104, Project Definition Phase (PDP) contracts were issued to Fairchild-Republic, McDonnell Douglas, and North American Rockwell on December 30, 1968. After considering the proposals advanced by all three firms, a design-and-development contract was issued to McDonnell Douglas for the aircraft that would be designated F-15.

The F-4 Phantom II was the USAF's most successful fighter during the Vietnam War but pointed to deficiencies in US strategy at the time, in that it was not optimized for close air-to-air combat under visual-engagement rules. Instead the aircraft had been conceived to use missiles at long range, rather than guns in close-range combat.

While contemplating the need for an aircraft capable of countering the MiG-25, the Air Force briefly considered a small, lightweight fighter along the lines of the F-104 Starfighter. The Starfighter had seen combat in Vietnam, but the Air Force considered this type of aircraft as having too many shortcomings to meet future needs.

CHAPTER 1

Procurement of the F-15 was such that no "XF-15" aircraft were built. Rather, the aircraft went from drawing board to production, with the first eighteen examples being Full Scale Development (FSD) aircraft. The first ten single-seat aircraft, serial numbers 71-0280 through 71-0289, were considered Category I test aircraft (as were two two-seat TF-15A aircraft, serial numbers 71-290 and 71-291), while the next eight aircraft, serial numbers 72-0113 through 72-0120, were considered Category II test aircraft. These initial production aircraft have been identified variously as F-15 FSD, YF-15A, F-15, and Cat I aircraft. In this volume, we use the YF-15A term for clarity.

The first of the aircraft, serial number 71-0280, rolled out of McDonnell Douglas's St. Louis plant on June 26, 1972. Owing in part to the urban nature of the St. Louis plant, the aircraft was subsequently dismantled and flown in the belly of a C-5 Galaxy to Edwards Air Force Base, California, where it was reassembled for its first flight. That flight occurred on July 27, 1972, with McDonnell Douglas chief test pilot Irving Burrows at the controls.

Powered by Pratt & Whitney F100 engines, providing a thrust-to-weight ratio greater than 1:1, the first flight was without hitch except for a minor problem with a landing-gear door. During the first flight, altitude was limited to 12,000 feet and speed to 250 knots. Subsequent flights gave a fuller appreciation of the type's capabilities. By late October 1973, eleven of the test aircraft were flying, and altitudes of 60,000 feet and speeds of Mach 2.3 had been reached. Few problems had been discovered, those being confined to buffeting, which were corrected by the removal of a diagonal area from the wingtip, and the necessity of increasing the area of the air brake substantially.

Development

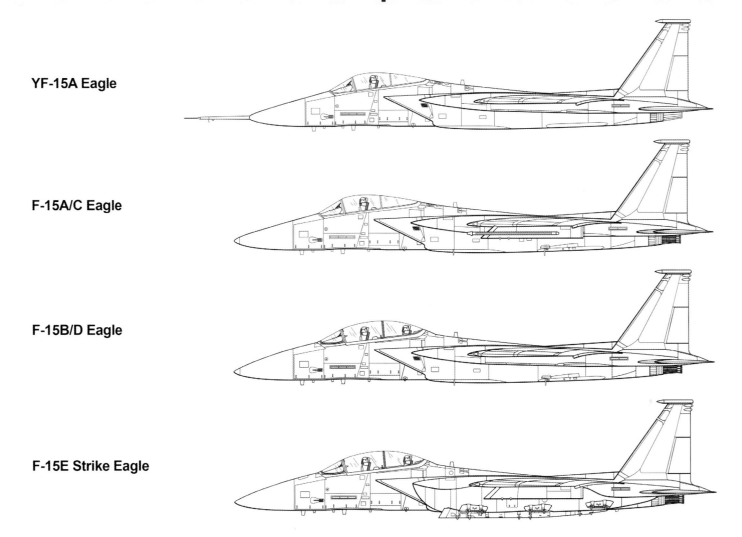

YF-15A Eagle

F-15A/C Eagle

F-15B/D Eagle

F-15E Strike Eagle

The first of the Eagles was F-15A, USAF serial number 71-0280, one of twelve Category 1 (contractor development, test, and evaluation) F-15s that McDonnell Douglas produced. This plane is shown being rolled out of the St. Louis factory on June 24, 1972. *National Archives*

The first F-15A Eagle is viewed from a different perspective on the occasion of its official rollout on June 24, 1972. The F-15s were designed with provisions to mount two AIM-7 Sparrow missiles on each side of the fuselage, and mockups of these are present. *National Archives*

The first F-105A, serial number 71-0280, appears here in a fairly fresh coat of paint, most likely Air Superiority Blue. Aside from stencils, the only markings are the national insignia, and "USAF" over "10280" on the vertical tail. The original, small speed brake is open. *National Museum of the United States Air Force*

After being rolled out in St. Louis, the first F-15A was partially disassembled and transported by C-5 Galaxy transport to Edwards Air Force Base for testing. The plane is shown here after arriving at Edwards on July 11, 1972, sixteen days before its first flight. *National Archives*

The first YF-15A is parked at the McDonnell Douglas plant in St. Louis, Missouri. After serving as a test plane, YF-15A, serial number 71-0280, had a second career, traveling around the United States as a static-display recruiting tool for the Air Force.

The first Eagle, the YF-15A with USAF serial number 71-0280, is shown in its early Air Superiority Blue paint job with Day-Glo orange trim. By the time this photo was taken, the intense sun of Edwards Air Force Base evidently had faded the orange to yellow. *National Museum of the United States Air Force*

An early YF-15A test plane is armed with cluster bombs and AIM-7 and AIM-9 missiles. On the nose is an air-data boom, with sensors for monitoring angle of attack, angle of sideslip, static pressure, total pressure, outside air temperature, and total air temperature. *National Museum of the United States Air Force*

YF-15A, serial number 71-0280, was painted overall in Air Superiority Blue, with areas of Day-Glo Orange. Marked on each side of the nose and the vertical tails were a stylized F-15 silhouette and the McDonnell Douglas logo. "EAGLE" also was marked on the nose. *National Museum of the United States Air Force*

Details of the layout of the Day-Glo orange paint on the first YF-15A, serial number 71-0280, are apparent on this view from below during flight. Initially, the first YF-15As had squared wingtips and straight leading edges on the horizontal stabilizers. *National Museum of the United States Air Force*

YF-15A, USAF serial number 71-0280, is viewed from the right side during an early test flight, showing the Day-Glo orange areas on the vertical tail, the horizontal stabilizer, the side of the engine intakes, the wing, and the air-data boom. *National Museum of the United States Air Force*

The first YF-15A is viewed from the upper right, providing more details of the Day-Glo orange areas. A close inspection of these photos of YF-15A 71-0280 reveals that the Day-Glo paint was not applied to the leading edges of the wings, fins, and stabilizers. *National Museum of the United States Air Force*

During a test flight, McDonnell Douglas YF-15A-3-MC, serial number 71-0286, is carrying Mk. 82 500-pound bombs on multiple-ejector racks. This Eagle was assigned to the combined McDonnell Douglas / US Air Force F-15 Joint Test Force at Edwards Air Force Base, California, from September 1973 to November 1980, where it was used as a test aircraft for armament development and external fuel stores. By the 1990s, it was displayed at the Octave Chanute Aerospace Museum, Rantoul, Illinois, and it later found a new home at the Saint Louis Science Center. *National Museum of the United States Air Force*

An early, test-model YF-15A is flying in formation below a Boeing KC-97 Stratofreighter during an aerial-refueling exercise in September 1974. The YF-15As and subsequent models had an air-refueling receptacle on the top of the left wing, near the wing root. *National Museum of the United States Air Force*

YF-15A-4-MC, serial number 71-0287, approaches Boeing KC-135A-BN Stratotanker, serial number 55-3135, for refueling. This Eagle first flew on August 25, 1973, and was employed in spin-recovery and angle-of-attack trials and in fuel-system testing. *National Museum of the United States Air Force*

YF-15A, serial number 71-0287, makes a landing approach with its dive brake extended; the spin-chute container is visible between the engine nozzles, painted in Day-Glo orange and black-and-white checkers. A large dive brake has replaced the original, smaller one. *National Museum of the United States Air Force*

In this photo of the first YF-15A, the Day-Glo orange areas on the upper surfaces are still quite fresh; later, these areas became faded where they were exposed directly to the sun. This YF-15A was used for envelope exploration, testing handling, and external stores. *National Museum of the United States Air Force*

During flight testing of the YF-15A, wing buffeting was encountered; the fix was to rake the wingtip. Further, after the first three YF-15A test planes experienced flutter, the straight leading edges of the stabilators received a notched, "dogtooth" design.

Wingtip Development

YF-15

Straight wingtip

F-15A

Raked wingtip with 4 square feet (0.4 square meters) removed from prototype wingtip

Elevon Development

YF-15

Notch cut into leading edge

F-15A

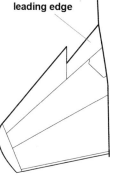

The YF-15A and subsequent models of the Eagle have separate, articulated intakes for the two engines. These are located to the sides of the cockpit, as seen in a photo of the first YF-15A. This plane lacked the production F-15s' M61 cannon in the right wing root. *National Museum of the United States Air Force*

The instrument panel in the cockpit of a YF-15A at Edwards Air Force Base on March 20, 1975, varied considerably from the Category 1 preproduction YF-15As. At the upper center of the instrument panel are communications and heads-up-display controls. *National Archives*

The cockpit of a YF-15A is viewed from a slightly different perspective in an April 1975 photo. At the bottom center is the control stick, on the grip of which were autopilot, weapons, trim, nose-gear, trigger, air-fueling-release, and weapons-release switches. *National Archives*

24

The left console of a YF-15A under evaluation at Edwards Air Force Base is seen on March 20, 1975. The console included communications controls and the throttle lever, on which were switches for systems such as the speed brakes and rudder trim. *National Archives*

The right console of the YF-15A includes the oxygen regulator, control panels for the engine, navigation, compass, environmental-control system, lights, and the tactical electronic-warfare system (TEWS). In the foreground is the Escapac IC-7 ejection seat. *National Archives*

The thirteenth preproduction YF-15A, USAF serial number 72-0115, was used for operational testing. Here, it is loaded with blue and Olive Drab practice bombs and inert AIM-9L Sidewinder missiles. Orange-colored pylons at various points hold orange cameras for documenting the test-firing of the plane's air-to-air missiles. Placed at intervals on the wings and the fuselage are black-and-white photo-reference markings. Numerous photo-reference markings are also on the bomb pylons.
National Museum of the United States

CHAPTER 2
F-15A and B Eagles

Delivery of Eagles to operational USAF units began in November 1974, with deliveries to the 555th Tactical Fighter Training Squadron of the 58th Tactical Training Wing at Luke AFB, Arizona. In January 1976, F-15A aircraft were delivered to the 1st Tactical Fighter Wing at Langley Air Force Base, Virginia, marking the initial delivery to a combat wing.

Once fielded, problems began to surface with the F100 engines. Redesign of some components as well as changes to the maintenance cycle resolved these problems; however, a less serious engine problem was introduced. That was a shortage of engines, a result of the aforementioned issues coupled with strikes at component manufacturers, which led to McDonnell Douglas delivering and the Air Force accepting aircraft without engines.

The F-15s went next on strength with the 32nd Tactical Fighter Wing, which was under control of the Dutch air force while fulfilling its NATO mission. Also equipped with the Eagle was the 33rd Tactical Fighter Wing at Eglin Air Force Base. A few interceptor squadrons attached to the Tactical Air Command exchanged their F-106 Delta Darts for the new McDonnell fighter as well.

The F-15B was initially designated the TF-15; the aircraft was the two-seat training version of the Eagle. With the same overall dimensions as the F-15A, the F-15B differed chiefly by having a larger canopy enclosing a second seat. In order to make room for the second seat, the fuel tank size was reduced slightly and the Internal Countermeasure Set (ICS) was not installed. No changes were made to the armament, and the performance of the aircraft was essentially the same as that of the F-15A.

The first flight of an F-15B, then designated TF-15A, was made by serial number 71-0290 on October 18, 1973. One TF-15A was built for every six F-15A aircraft. The first TF-15A delivery to an operational USAF unit occurred on November 4, 1974, when serial number 73-0108 was turned over to the 555th Tactical Fighter Training Squadron of the 58th Tactical Training Wing at Luke AFB, Arizona. President Gerald Ford was the keynote speaker for the occasion.

Following the initial test program, the first two TF-15A aircraft, serial numbers 71-0290 and 71-0291, were later modified for use in further development of the Eagle. Aircraft 71-0290 was modified for use as part of the Short Takeoff and Landing (STOL) program and the Maneuver Technology Demonstrator (Agile Eagle) program. The second aircraft was used in the evaluation of the FAST Pack conformal fuel tanks and LANTIRN pod prior to becoming the development aircraft for the F-15E Strike Eagle. Other F-15B aircraft produced were 73-108 through 73-114, 74-137 through 74-142, 75-080 through 75-089, 76-124 through 76-142, and 77-154 through 77-168. Serial numbers 76-1524 and 76-1525 were delivered to the Israeli air force.

By 1982, the F-15A (and B) was beginning to show its age. A multistage improvement program (MSIP) was developed that would significantly improve the aircraft. However, this project was subsequently canceled, with cost being cited as the reason. Instead, the aircraft were given more-modest upgrades utilizing a portion of a similar program developed for the F-15C/D.

Following McDonnell Douglas's and the Air Force's successful testing of the preproduction YF-15As, full production of the single-seat F-15As and the two-seat F-15Bs began at McDonnell Douglas's St. Louis plant. A total of 384 F-15As were completed. Shown here is F-15A-11-MC, USAF serial number 74-0100, one of eighteen planes completed in the -11 production block. There were consecutively numbered production blocks for the F-15A from 1 to 20. The "MC" suffix pertains to McDonnell Douglas. The "FF" tail code represented the 1st Tactical Fighter Wing. *National Museum of the United States Air Force*

Among the twelve Category 1 preproduction F-15s was a pair of two-seater F-15Bs, USAF serial numbers 71-0290 and, *seen here*, 71-0291. Originally designated TF-15A, the F-15B was intended as a training aircraft, with flight controls in the rear cockpit. *National Museum of the United States Air Force*

F-15A-15-MC, USAF serial number 76-0043, is seen from the upper right front with its access doors open and access panels removed. The doors along the front of the fuselage had recessed latch handles. In the right wing root is the one gun installed in the F-15A: the M61A1 Vulcan 20 mm gun, a rotary, six-barreled, Gatling-type cannon with a rate of fire of 4,000 or 6,000 rounds per minute. The speed brake, which on production F-15s has approximately 50 percent more area than those of the preproduction F-15s, is extended. *National Museum of the United States Air Force*

The antenna of the AN/APG-63 radar is viewed from the front, with the radome swung to the right side. A strut at the bottom of the radome locks it into the open position, and a strut is also used to hold the radar electronics-bay door in the open position.

There were many access panels and doors on the F-15A to allow ground crews and technicians to work on the complex interior systems of the plane. Those doors and panels have been removed or swung open in this photograph. At the front is the open radome for the Hughes AN/APG-63 radar. The two upward-opening doors to the rear of the radar antenna housed radar electronics boxes. Those doors themselves held the pitot tubes and contained the forward antennas for the AN/ALQ-128 Electronic Warfare Warning Set.

With the radome and the access doors open, the antenna of the Hughes AN/APG-63 radar is visible to the left. To the rear of it are bays containing electronics for the radar, such as the power supply, wave-guide assemblies, radar transmitter, and data processor.

The radome of the F-15A, seen here open, comprised a synthetic-foam core within an inner and outer skin. The radome was able to withstand temperatures up to 500 degrees Fahrenheit. "RADIATION HAZARD" is painted on the front of the radar antenna.

The dual-engine F-15A poses next to its smaller, single-engine stablemate in the USAF air-superiority-fighter inventory, the General Dynamics F-16 Fighting Falcon. The F-15A entered operational service in November 1974, almost four years before the F-16. *National Museum of the United States Air Force*

This view from below of an F-15A in flight provides a clear idea of the shape of the raked wingtips and the notched leading edges of the stabilators. On the centerline pylon is a 610-gallon auxiliary fuel tank. The titanium skin around the rears of the engines was left unpainted. The fuselage extensions to the outboard sides of the engine nozzles also were bare metal except for the rear tips. *National Museum of the United States Air Force*

The design of the F-15A was all about graceful contours and smart streamlining, as evidenced in a view over the left engine intake facing aft. In the rear are the bulged fairings that enclosed the rears of the jet engines. The curved fairing at the front of the wing root is called the glove; on this side of the F-15A, the air-refueling receptacle is housed inside the glove, with a door over the receptacle. On the deck to the rear of the cockpit canopy is a UHF/VHF blade antenna.

With sheaves of checklists and manuals in hand, an F-15A pilot stands poised at the bottom of the boarding ladder for the cockpit in this undated photograph. The national insignia used at the time, partially visible behind the boarding ladder, featured a blue circle with white star and red and white bars to the sides, with no blue borders around the bars. The number 7118 is stenciled in black vertically on the nose-gear door. *National Museum of the United States Air Force*

An F-15A undergoes climatic testing in a simulated tropical environment in a hangar at McKinley Climatic Laboratory, Eglin Air Force Base, Florida, in 1975. A flexible hose from the test cart is plugged into the ground-cooling receptacle on the fuselage. *National Museum of the United States Air Force*

The same F-15A depicted in the preceding photo is towed out of the McKinley Climatic Laboratory following a two-month period of climatic tests to establish the plane's ability to withstand extremes of atmospheric conditions. *National Museum of the United States Air Force*

This view of technicians aligning the heads-up display (HUD) around August 1973 offers a good view of the top of the fuselage and wings aft of the cockpit. The speed brake is the original design, found on preproduction and very early F-15As. *National Museum of the United States Air Force*

Escapac IC-7   **McDonnell Douglas ACES II**

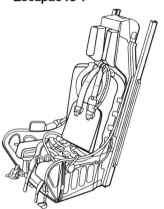
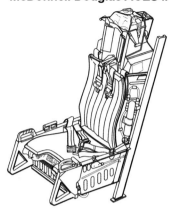

Eagle prototypes and early F-15As and F-15Bs had the Douglas IC-7 Escapac ejection seat. Escapac seats were later replaced by the McDonnell Douglas ACES II ejection seat. A key difference between these types was that the Escapac had a pull ring at the center front of the seat cushion to eject the seat, while the ACES II had a pull ring on each side.

The F-15B featured a new canopy that was slightly enlarged at the rear to accommodate the rear seat. The second F-15B, again shown here, had markings for "F-15," a silhouette of the plane, and the McDonnell Douglas logo on the nose and the vertical tails. *National Museum of the United States Air Force*

An F-15B is lining up for an aerial refueling. The plane is painted in overall Air Superiority Blue, which was used on the earliest F-15s. Later, this F-15B would receive a red, white, and blue scheme similar to one intended for the USAF Thunderbirds. *National Museum of the United States Air Force*

McDonnell Douglas F-15A-18-MC, serial number 77-0068 and manufacturer's serial number 0342/A280, is on static display at Arnold Air Force Base, Tullahoma, Tennessee. It is painted in a dark-gray over light-gray air-superiority camouflage scheme.

Before being displayed at Arnold Air Force Base, F-15A-18-MC, serial number 77-0068, had been on display, successively, in the 1990s, at the National Museum of the US Air Force and at Rickenbacker Airport, Columbus, Ohio. *Author*

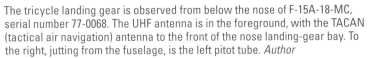

The tricycle landing gear is observed from below the nose of F-15A-18-MC, serial number 77-0068. The UHF antenna is in the foreground, with the TACAN (tactical air navigation) antenna to the front of the nose landing-gear bay. To the right, jutting from the fuselage, is the left pitot tube. *Author*

The nose landing gear is seen from the left side, showing the taxi light (*upper*) and landing light (*lower*) and the retraction strut. The aft door of the landing-gear bay is linked to the oleo strut of the landing gear. *Author*

The nose-gear oleo strut and taxi and landing lights are viewed close-up from the right front. The landing gear was retracted hydraulically, with electrical controls.

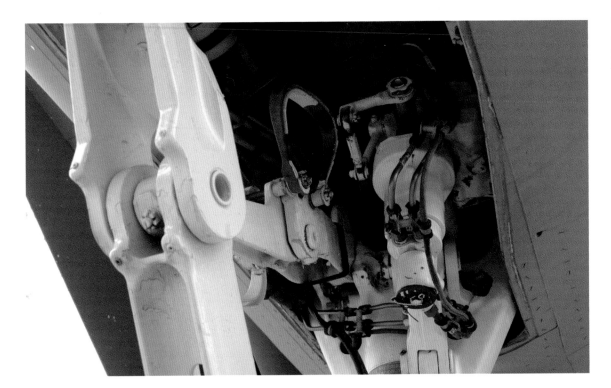

The retraction strut (*left*) and the upper works of the nose landing gear are viewed from the left front. *Author*

The upper part of the nose-gear retraction strut is observed close-up from the right side. *Author*

The aft part of the nose landing-gear bay is seen, facing aft, from the front, with the retraction strut to the far right and the upper part of the nose gear toward the bottom right. *Author*

The windscreen of the F-15A was formed from an outer and an inner surface of fusion-bonded cast acrylic, with a center layer of polycarbonate. This laminate was resistant to bird strikes. The cockpit canopy was of polycarbonate with an abrasion-resistant coating. *Author*

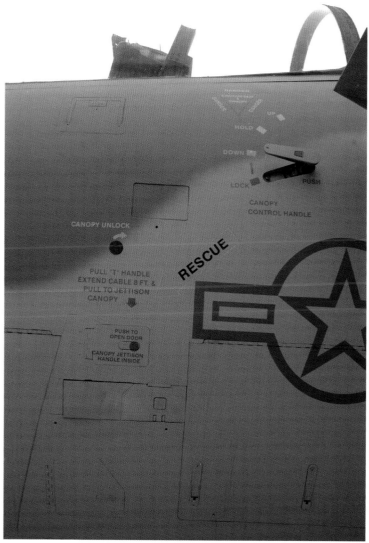

Below the red canopy-unlock button, and indicated by a "RESCUE" marker, is a small door, inside of which is a T-handle for jettisoning the canopy. To effect an emergency jettisoning of the canopy, a button on the door was pressed to open it, and the T-handle and cable were pulled out 8 feet. *Author*

On the fuselage on the left side of the cockpit are, *at bottom*, the red-colored canopy unlock button, and, *right of center*, the exterior canopy-control handle. The handle is in the "down" position. Prior to flight, the handle was rotated full left and pushed in, to store it in its recess. By rotating the handle to the right, there was a "hold" position and an "open" position. *Author*

On the left side of the forward fuselage are, *left to right*, the pitot tube, the spike-shaped angle-of-attack sensor, a low-voltage formation-light strip, and, *to the far right*, the canopy-release handle in its extended position. *Author*

In a view into the left engine-air intake, at the top of the intake are two adjustable ramps, to regulate shock waves and improve engine efficiency. *Author*

The engine-air intakes of the F-15s have a pivoting, variable-geometry feature, enabling them to tilt downward, to optimize the flow of air into the engines during subsonic flight. The pivot points are the rounded features near the bottom of the intake. *Author*

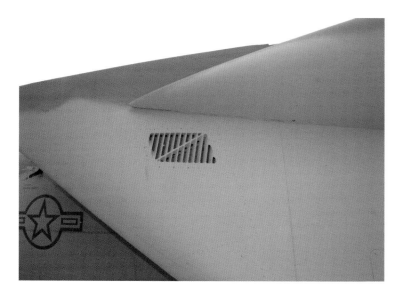

On the side of the left engine-air intake, below the wing glove, is a bleed-air duct, which conducts excess air out of the intake. *Author*

On each side of the fuselage are two stations for mounting missiles. This is the forward left station. The missile is fastened to the fitting in the foreground, and the C-shaped sway brace in the background helps hold the missile in position until it is fired. The unit crest is for the 46th Test Wing. *Author*

The right rear fuselage missile station is equipped with a strake, above the sway bar, to ensure a clean separation of the missile from the aircraft when fired. *Author*

The right main landing gear is viewed from the outboard side. When the gear was lowered, only the small door adjacent to the oleo strut was open. Like the nose landing gear, the main landing gear retracted forward into its bays. *Author*

A closer view of the right main landing gear shows the retraction strut. Below that strut's junction with the oleo strut is the antitorque "scissors" link. *Author*

The left main landing gear is observed from the right rear, showing the brake. The landing gear is secured by a cable to a pad eye on the pavement next to the tire. *Author*

Details of the left landing gear are displayed, including the oleo strut, retraction strut, antitorque link, and inner side of the aft landing-gear-bay door. The dark rectangle on the door is an instructional plate concerning the hydraulic system. *Author*

The port for the M61A1 Vulcan cannon, on the leading edge of the right wing glove, is of shiny, bare titanium. Also referred to as a nozzle, the port was designed to exclude gases produced by the firing of the gun, which could cause the plane to stall. To the lower front of the port is a bleed-air duct. *Author*

On the right wingtip, as seen from below, is the navigation light, with a green lens, next to which is the dome-shaped AN/ALR-56 ECM antenna. *Author*

As seen from the rear of the right wing, on the trailing edge of the wingtip to the right of the aileron is an oblong opening, the fuel jettison pipe. The marking on the center of the aileron is a "honeycomb" design of interlocked hexagons with "NO STEP" printed on them. *Author*

As viewed from behind the left afterburner exhaust nozzle, the rear of the fuselage transitions to two tail booms, the inner side of the left one being shown. The tail booms support the vertical tails. A simple bracket has been attached to the bottom of the rudder and the vertical fin, to immobilize the rudder. *Author*

On the bottom of each side of the fuselage is an exhaust vent for a heat exchanger. The openings in the rears of the vents are approximately in line with the trailing edges of the wings. The underside of the fuselage in this area was left unpainted. *Author*

The right vertical tail is observed from the front of the right stabilator. To the left is the "dogtooth," a jog in the leading edge of the aileron. The positions of the tiger-stripes and thunderbolt motifs on the right vertical tail are reversed from those on the left tail, with the thunderbolt being on the bottom. *Author*

The variable-area convergent-divergent afterburner exhaust nozzles of the Pratt & Whitney F100 turbofan engines of F-15A-18-MC, serial number 77-0068, are viewed from the left rear, with the right vertical tail and tail boom in the background. *Author*

McDonnell Douglas F-15A-7-MC, serial number 73-0085 and manufacturer's number 0023/A019, is preserved at the Museum of Aviation, Warner Robins Air Force Base, Georgia. With the canopy open, a partial view of the cockpit, the heads-up display, and the ejection seat is available. *Author*

To the rear of the cockpit canopy is the air-conditioning cooling-air exhaust vent. Aft of that vent are a UHF antenna and, on the air brake, a strake, a reinforcing feature on very early F-15As. On the upper surface of the wing glove are the cooling-air vent (*front*) and exhaust (*rear*) grilles for the M61A1 Vulcan cannon. Between the wing glove and the canopy are, *front to rear*, an engine intake bleed vent; the intake-bypass air-spill duct, the door of which is open; and the intake duct air-bleed louver. *Author*

Both wings are in view, with "NO STEP" stencils at various places on them. The strake on the air brake is evident. *Author*

AIM-9L Sidewinder training missiles are mounted on the left pylon of F-15A-7-MC, serial number 73-0085. Red "REMOVE TO ARM" tags are attached to the missiles and launchers. AIM-7 Sparrow air-to-air missiles are installed on the fuselage launcher stations. *Author*

The two AIM-9L training missiles on the left pylon are viewed from nearly head-on. To the far left, on the leading edge of the wing, is a collision light with a red lens. *Author*

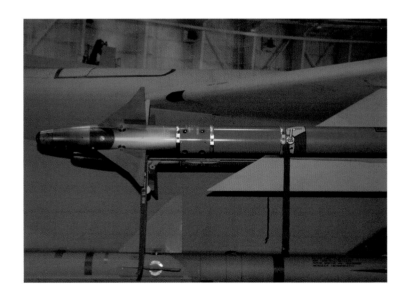

The blue finish on the AIM-9L Sidewinders indicates that they are for training purposes. The front fins, called canards, were steerable. The red tag to the right is attached to the safe/arm control. *Author*

The left pylon is viewed from the left rear, showing the aft part of the AIM-9L Sidewinder training missile and the rear of the launcher-rail assembly. On the outer rear corners of each rear fin is a gyroscopic device known as a rolleron, which incorporates an air-driven wheel that prevents the missile from rolling. *Author*

The centerline pylon with the 610-gallon external fuel tank, *left*, and the right main landing gear, *right*, are observed from the rear. Both the pylon and the external fuel tank were equipped with pivot points, *visible here*, for ensuring the structures made a clean exit from the aircraft when jettisoned. *Author*

The right underwing pylon and an external fuel tank of an F-15A at the National Museum of the US Air Force are observed from the right rear. Pivot points are on the upper aft corner of the pylon as well as on the junction of the pylon and the fin of the external fuel tank, to ensure that both structures would make a clean exit from the aircraft if jettisoned. *Author*

The F-15A displayed at the Museum of Aviation, at Warner Robbins Air Force Base, is equipped with "turkey feathers" on its exhaust nozzles. A feature on early F-15As, turkey feathers consisted of seventeen titanium flaps, designed to protect the nozzle actuators. Turkey feathers were discontinued on F-15As because of their high cost and the trouble to maintain them. *Author*

An example of an F-15A with the turkey feathers removed from the exhaust nozzles is displayed at the National Museum of the US Air Force. The flaps of the nozzles were operated by pneumatic power, using bleed air from the engines. Details of the afterburner are visible inside the nozzles. Between the nozzles is the arrestor hook. *Author*

Details of the interior of the cockpit canopy are seen from the right side, including the hooks for locking the canopy in the closed position, and the cross-members, with lightening holes, for supporting the deck in the rear of the canopy. Behind the ejector seat is a red brace, manually inserted to support the canopy when open. The actuator for the canopy is farther to the rear. *Author*

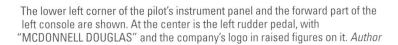

The lower left corner of the pilot's instrument panel and the forward part of the left console are shown. At the center is the left rudder pedal, with "MCDONNELL DOUGLAS" and the company's logo in raised figures on it. *Author*

The F-15A had a conventional instrument panel; multipurpose displays would come later, with the F-15E. The round instrument to the upper right is the TEWS display, to the left of which is the heads-up-display control panel. To the rear of the instrument panel is the pilot's control stick. On the front of the right console are oxygen controls and cabin climate controls. *Author*

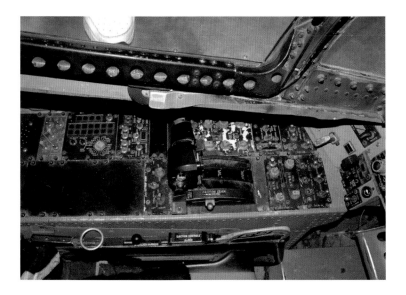

On the left console are the throttle controls, as well as control panels for systems such as TACAN, instrument-landing system, external fuel tanks, anticollision lights, and ground power. The yellow left handle for initiating seat ejection is to the left side of the seat. *Author*

Some of the features on the right console include the oxygen regulator, ECS (environmental-control system) controls, cabin temperature panel, engine control panel, navigation control panel, interior lights controls, and oxygen hose and oxygen outlet panel. The area at the rear of the console is for stowage. *Author*

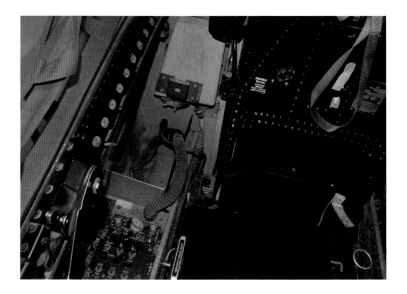

In a view looking to the rear in the cockpit of the F-15A, to the left is the rear part of the right console, and to the right is the black-colored ejection seat. At the center is the pilot's oxygen hose. *Author*

A close-up view shows parts of the ejection seat and the rear of the left console. Near the rear of the console is the anti-G panel, with a hose and coupling. The bright-green bottle on the side of the ejection seat contained emergency oxygen. Affixed to the seat back is a data plate, which includes such information as the name of the manufacturer, the part number and serial number, and the contract number. *Author*

A zoom image of F-15A-7-MC, serial number 73-0085, at the Museum of Aviation, Warner Robins Air Force Base, shows the open canopy, with three rearview mirrors on the front frame. Parts of the avionics bay, to the rear of the cockpit, are visible. In early F-15s, the avionics bay was painted a metallic blue green, as is the case here. *Author*

Specifications

	F-15A	F-15C	F-15E
DIMENSIONS			
Wingspan	42', 9.75"	42', 9.75"	42', 9.75"
Length	63', 9"	63', 9"	63', 9"
Height	18', 5.5"	18', 5.5"	18', 5.5"
FUEL			
Integral	11,908 lbs.	13,771 lbs.	13,432 lbs.
External (max.)	11,895 lbs.	36,200 lbs.	36,200 lbs.
In-flight refueling	yes	yes	yes
WEIGHTS			
Empty weight	28,600 lbs.	28,600 lbs.	31,700 lbs.
Maximum gross weight	68,000 lbs.	68,000 lbs.	81,000 lbs.
PERFORMANCE			
Maximum speed	1,650 mph @36,000'	1,650 mph @36,000'	1,650 mph @40,000'
Service ceiling	60,000'	60,000'	60,000'
Range, w/external tanks	2,878 miles	2,878 miles	2,878 miles
Range, w/conformal tanks	N/A	3,450 miles	3,570 miles
ENGINES			
Type	2 x Pratt & Whitney F100-PW-100	2 x Pratt & Whitney F100-PW-220	2 x Pratt & Whitney F100-PW-229
Maximum thrust	23,450 lbs. each	23,450 lbs. each	29,000 lbs. each
COST	$27.9 million each	$29.9 million each	$31.1 million each
ARMAMENT			
Cannon	1 × M61A1 20 mm Vulcan	1 × M61A1 20 mm Vulcan	1 × M61A1 20 mm Vulcan
Ammunition	940 rounds	940 rounds	940 rounds
Missile	4 × AIM-9 Sidewinder, up to four AIM-7 Sparrow or AIM-120 AMRAAM	4 × AIM-9 Sidewinder, up to four AIM-7 Sparrow or AIM-120 AMRAAM	4 × AIM-9 Sidewinder, up to four AIM-7 Sparrow or 8 AIM-120 AMRAAM

CHAPTER 3

F-15C, F-15D, and F-15J Eagle

The introduction of the F-15C, first flown on February 16, 1979, lessened the amount of maintenance required, by deletion of the trouble-prone "turkey feathers" that covered the variable exhaust nozzles of the engines on the F-15A from the onset of production. These were also removed from the F-15As in the field. Compared to its predecessor, the electronics suite of the F-15C showed several improvements, most notably a programmable signal processor, which allowed for rapid switching of the radar between modes.

The F-15C also introduced the "FAST" (fuel and sensor tactical) packs to the airframe. Attached to the fuselage outside each air intake, these tanks conform to the aerodynamic shape of the fuselage, increasing fuel capacity with little change in aircraft performance. Now known as conformal fuel tanks (CFT), these tanks, though rarely taken off, can be removed by ground crews in about fifteen minutes. The tanks have a capacity of 849 gallons, although by reducing the amount of fuel equipment such as cameras, radar jammers, laser designators, and infrared equipment can be carried.

A further increase in range was achieved by the addition of internal-wing leading- and trailing-edge fuel tanks, as well as additional tankage inside the fuselage. The internal fuel capacity of the F-15C is 2,070 gallons, which could be augmented by the FAST packs as well as three external drop tanks. The extra fuel meant that the F-15C had a considerably higher gross weight than the F-15A, requiring redesigned landing gear and tires, changes that are noticeable to the observer. The USAF purchased 408 F-15Cs by the time production ended in 1985.

At the same time that the F-15C was introduced to replace the F-15A, the F-15D was introduced as a replacement for the F-15B. The first flight of an F-15D occurred on June 19, 1979. Dimensionally the F-15D was the same size as the F-15C and has similar performance, but it lacked the internal ALQ-135 electronic countermeasures (ECM) system. The USAF purchased sixty-one F-15Ds for its own use, while a further sixteen were built for Saudi Arabia.

The F-15C improved on the F-15A in several respects. The F-15C carried 280 more gallons internally, had provisions for mounting conformal fuel tanks, and featured improved electronic countermeasures (ECM) equipment and a stronger airframe. The Escapac IC-7 ejection seat of the preproduction and early F-15A/B had been replaced following Block 16 by the ACES II ejection seat. After F-15C production commenced, further improvements were made to the plane. The F-15C first flew on February 26, 1979. This photo shows the first of the C-model Eagles, the F-15C-21-MC with serial number 78-0468, with "F-15C," the McDonnell Douglas logo, and "NO. 1" marked on the nose. *National Museum of the United States Air Force*

As the F-15A has a two-seat version, the F-15B, the F-15C's two-seat version is the F-15D. The US Air Force received sixty-one of them, and thirty-six were distributed to Israel, Japan, and Saudi Arabia. This example, F-15D-25-MC, USAF serial number 79-009, bears tail markings for the 54th Fighter Squadron (yellow stripe), 3rd Wing ("AK"), 11th Air Force, based at Elmendorf Air Force Base, Alaska. On the inside of the left vertical tail is a representation of the Big Dipper and the North Star. *Dana Bell*

F-15C-21-MC, serial number 78-0468, is viewed from the upper right during a test flight. The F-15s followed a serial production-block numbering system from model to model: the -21 suffix for the first block of F-15Cs followed the -20 block number of the previous batch of F-15Bs. *National Museum of the United States Air Force*

The first F-15C, serial number 79-0468, undergoes a test flight, armed with AIM-7 Sparrow missiles. Visible below the rear of the fuselage are two orange-colored cameras and mounts for documenting the test-firing of the air-to-air missiles. *National Museum of the United States Air Force*

F-15C-24-MC, USAF serial number 79-0015, is carrying a full complement of four AIM-7 Sparrow air-to-air, radar-homing missiles on the fuselage and four AIM-9 Sidewinder short-range air-to-air missiles on launcher rails on the pylons. A 610-gallon auxiliary fuel tank is on the centerline hardpoints. The "CR" tail code represents the 32nd Tactical Fighter Squadron. *National Museum of the United States Air Force*

An F-15C is viewed from the front, with conformal fuel tanks on carts to the sides, in an April 1983 photograph. Originally known as FAST (fuel and sensor tactical) tanks but now called conformal fuel tanks (CFTs), they could be attached to or removed from the sides of the fuselage as the mission dictated. Each tank added 849 US gallons of fuel to the F-15C's total capacity. Pylons were built into the CFTs to accept bombs or AIM-7 Sparrows. *National Museum of the United States Air Force*

The first F-15C is undergoing a test flight equipped with CFTs, with twelve Mk. 82 500-pound, low-drag, general-purpose (LDGP) bombs mounted on the CFTs. Black-and-white photo-reference stickers have been applied to the plane for the tests. *National Museum of the United States Air Force*

The lines of the F-15C, which
entered production in 1978, were
essentially the same as for the
F-15A. Most of the differences
were in improved systems,
including a strengthened landing
gear, a new digital central
computer, provisions for conformal
fuel tanks, and the new APG-63
radar, with a revolutionary, new
programmable signal processor
that, among other things, allowed
for progressive upgrades in the
weapons suite.

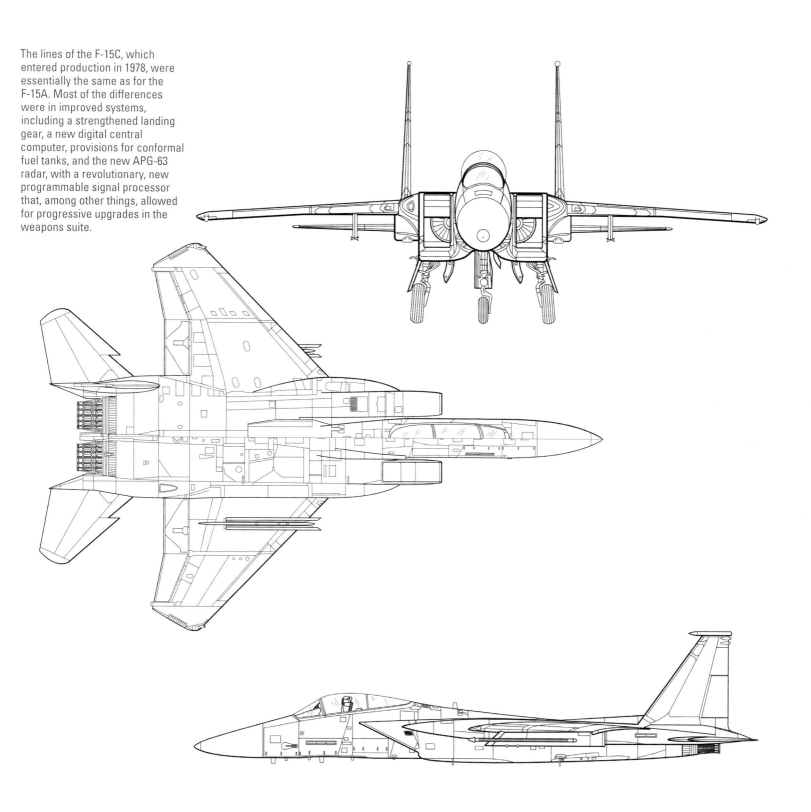

F-15D-36-MC, serial number 83-050, of the 27th Tactical Fighter Squadron, 1st Tactical Fighter Wing, is parked next to another F-15 at a desert base in March 1991. On the side of the engine air inlet trunk is the insignia of the 1st TFW. The number 3050 is marked just aft of the radome. *Dana Bell*

The F-15D was created to serve as the two-seat trainer version of the F-15C. As such, it featured all the improvements incorporated into the F-15C airframe, albeit with reduced internal fuel capacity. The two-place cockpit is shown to good advantage in this photo of NASA F-15D 897, taken on November 10, 2015. *NASA*

McDonnell Douglas F-15D-34-MC, serial number 82-046, of the 27th Tactical Fighter Squadron (yellow tail band), 1st Tactical Air Wing ("FF" tail code), is parked in a revetment while based in Saudi Arabia around early 1991. AIM-9 Sidewinders are mounted on the pylons.

In December 1975 the Japanese Defense Agency adopted the F-15 as the replacement for the nation's fleet of F-4EJ Phantom IIs. Two models were initially procured, the F-15C-based F-15J and the F-15D-based F-15DJ. Except for the first two F-15Js and twelve F-15DJs, the aircraft would be produced in Japan by Mitsubishi. Here, Senior Airman Carolyn Liddiard gives hand signals to the pilot of a McDonnell Douglas–built F-15J Eagle of the Japan Air Self-Defense Force (JASDF) while taxiing at Kadena Air Base, Okinawa, on April 23, 1981.

TSgt. Ronald J. Breemen, USAF, is peeling masking tape from the white border of a red hinomaru insignia on a US-built F-15 Eagle that is being prepared for transfer to the JASDF at Kadena Air Force Base, Okinawa, on March 24, 1981.

A JASDF F-15J pilot sits beneath the open canopy while parked on a rain-swept flight line at Nyūtabaru Air Base, Japan, during Exercise Cope North 86-4, a joint exercise of Pacific Rim allies, on September 11, 1986.

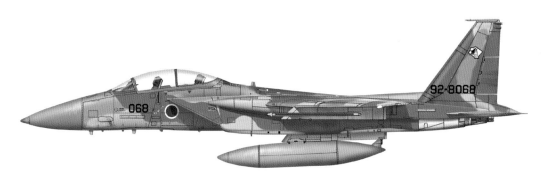

Two-seat Eagles in the JASDF are designated F-15DJ. This example, manufactured by Mitsubishi, bore JASDF serial number 92-8068 on the tail and was assigned to the JASDF's Aggressor Group (Hiko Kyodo-tai) at Nyūtabaru Air Base on the island of Kyūshū, Japan.

Two F-15J Eagle aircraft of the 202nd Tactical Fighter Squadron, JASDF, take off in formation during the joint US/Japan Exercise Cope North 85-4. The size of the JASDF's F-15 fleet is second only to the US Air Force in size.

JASDF's F-15J and F-15DJ aircraft approach a US Air Force KC-135 during aerial-refueling training on July 30, 1990. The training is in preparation for JASDF participation in Red Flag Alaska this year.

A JASDF F-15 flies alongside a US Air Force KC-135 from the 909th Air Refueling Squadron, Kadena Air Base, after being refueled during air refueling training on July 30, 1990. The training is in preparation for JASDF participation in Red Flag Alaska this year.

Al-Quwwât al-Jawwîyah as-Su'ûdîyah (the Royal Saudi Air Force: RSAF) has acquired numerous F-15s over the decades. This RSAF F-15C takes off during Operation Desert Shield.

This RSAF F-15C carries the tail number 1322. The tail numbers were the Saudis' own and did not directly correlate to USAF serial numbers. The RSAF insignia was on the side of the engine intake trunk, and the RSAF ensign was on the upper part of the vertical tail.

An RSAF F-15 Eagle fighter aircraft approaches a KC-135 Stratotanker from the 1700th Air Refueling Squadron (Provisional) for refueling during Operation Desert Shield.

McDonnell Douglas F-15C-32-MC, serial number 81-0048 and manufacturer's serial number 0801/C231, was photographed while assigned to the 95th Fighter Squadron, 325th Fighter Wing, at Tyndall Air Force Base, Florida. *Author*

A blue plastic cover marked "95FS" (95th Fighter Squadron) in white is secured over the right engine inlet of F-15C-32-MC, serial number 81-0048. Inside the windscreen is the heads-up display, with a cover installed over it. On the side of the engine inlet is the crest of the 325th Operations Group, to which the 95th Fighter Squadron has been assigned for many years.

Stencils are found sparingly on this F-15C. On the side of the radome, near its rear edge, is marked, "CAUTION CHECK ANTENNA POSITION PRIOR TO FULL EXTENSION OF RADOME." On the forward of the two dorsal blade antennas, the UHF antenna, "DO NOT PAINT" is marked in black. Just aft of that antenna is the TACOM antenna. *Author*

Below the windscreen is a pale-gray panel, edged with a checkerboard pattern. Below that, and casting a long shadow, is the right angle-of-attack sensor, below and to the rear of which is a low-voltage formation lighting strip. On the turtle deck to the rear of the cockpit canopy is a UHF blade antenna. The crest of the 95th Fighter Squadron is on the side of the engine intake. *Author*

The number 1048 on the inside of the nose landing-gear door is a truncated version of the plane's tail number, 81-0048. The taxi and landing lights on the nose landing gear have blue rims. *Author*

The tires on the F-15C are Michelin Aviators, size 34.5 × 9.75 – 18. The eight holes in the wheel assist with cooling the brake. Directly above the tire is the antitorque "scissors" link, which points forward, above which is the retraction strut. Extending forward from the oleo strut is the bungee cord that is holding the cover for the engine intake. *Author*

The left main landing gear, the 610-gallon external fuel tank, the left rear Sparrow missile-launcher unit, the left wing pylon, and part of the fuselage are in view. On the rear of the centerline pylon is a fitting, called a pivot point, which is attached to the small fin on the tank. This device allowed the tank to make a safe (for the aircraft) exit when jettisoned. *Author*

Details on the left wingtip of the F-15C include, *front to rear*, an electronic-countermeasures (ECM) antenna, with a white dome; the left navigation light, with a red lens; and a low-voltage formation light. Jutting from the top of the right vertical fin is a spike-shaped mass balance, also called the harmonic balancer. *Author*

The port for the M61A1 Vulcan 20 mm cannon is in the leading edge of the right wing glove, as viewed from alongside the front right of the fuselage. The dark shape on the leading edge of the wing near the cannon port is the lens for the right anticollision light. Below the wing is the left pylon, with a launcher on each side for an AIM-9 Sidewinder air-to-air missile. *Author*

Details of the left vertical fin and rudder of F-15C-32-MC, serial number 81-0048, are displayed. At the top of the fin is an electronic-warfare-system antenna. On the trailing edge of each fin is a radar-warning antenna. Below these antennas are, on the left fin, the tail navigation light, and on the right fin, an anticollision light. The top of the left tail is marked "MR BONES," and the top of the right tail "BONES 1." *Author*

The left side of F-15C-32-MC, serial number 81-0048, is observed from adjacent to the left tailplane. Aft of and below the right rudder is an internal countermeasures set (ICS) antenna, for jamming surface-to-air missile guidance systems. A similar antenna is below and aft of the left rudder and is hidden by the left tailplane. *Author*

CHAPTER 4
F-15E Strike Eagle and Derivatives

Under the project name Strike Eagle, McDonnell Douglas and Hughes Aircraft undertook a joint, self-funded project in the late 1970s to convert the second F-15B, serial number 71-0291, to a multirole Eagle specializing in ground attack, supplanting the aging F-111. The aircraft was initially known as the Advanced Fighter Capability Demonstrator, which then evolved as part of the Enhanced Tactical Fighter program, which in turn was renamed the Dual-Role Fighter.

To fill this need, the Advanced Fighter Capability F-15 was pitted against the Panavia Tornado and the F-16XL. On February 24, 1984, the US Air Force selected the F-15E to fill its requirements. Assembly of the first three F-15E aircraft began in July 1985, with the first of them, 86-0183, taking to the air initially on December 11, 1986. This aircraft utilized an older style of aft fuselage, but the next two examples were purely F-15E, and the first of those flew on March 31, 1987.

The first full-production F-15E was delivered to the 405th Tactical Training Wing at Luke Air Force Base in April 1988. Dubbed the Strike Eagle, the F-15E is equipped with conformal fuel tanks; a new radar, the AN/APG-70, with air-to-ground and air-to-air functions; and a rear cockpit outfitted for a weapon systems operator (WSO).

During the course of F-15E production, McDonnell Douglas merged with Boeing. While first proposed in late 1996, the deal was finalized in August 1997, through a stock swap. Boeing provided $13.3 billion in stock for the McDonnell stock. Although Boeing was the surviving name and provided the funding, strangely, shortly thereafter former McDonnell Douglas executives took the top positions at Boeing. In addition they became the largest individual shareholders.

Initially, the F-15E used the Pratt & Whitney F100-PW-220, but later production aircraft feature the more powerful P&W F100-PW-229 engines

In 2007, the radar of the F-15E was upgraded to the Raytheon APG-82 active electronically scanned array (AESA), which was initially known as the APG-63(V)4.

Longtime F-15 user Israel acquired their own version of the F-15E, the F-15I Ra'am ("Thunder"). The F-15I utilizes a different electronic suite, in part due to US State Department security restrictions.

In 1992, Saudi Arabia purchased seventy-two F-15E-derived F-15S aircraft through a program known as Peace Sun IX. These aircraft differ from the F-15E by having degraded electronics, again due to security restrictions. Delivery of these aircraft began on September 12, 1995, and was concluded on November 10, 1999.

In 2010, the Royal Saudi Arabian Air Force ordered eighty-four improved aircraft, which are designated F-15SA (Saudi Advanced). These aircraft feature a redesigned cockpit and APG-63(V)3 AESA radar, digital electronic-warfare systems (DEWS), and infrared search and track (IRST) systems. In addition, sixty-six of the nation's existing F-15S aircraft will be remanufactured to F-15SA standards, a process that will include replacing the wings and forward fuselage. The updated aircraft are referred to as F-15SR.

The Republic of Korea selected a derivative of the F-15E as its next-generation fighter in April 2002, placing a $4.2 billion, forty-aircraft order in June of that year. The aircraft are known as the F-15K Slam Eagle. The first two examples were delivered at the Seoul Air Show in October 2005, and the final deliveries under the contract were made in October 2008. However, a further twenty-one F-15K aircraft had been ordered in April 2008. At the time of their delivery, the F-15K were the most advanced Eagles to be fielded, and included a joint helmet-mounted cueing system (JHMCS).

On September 6, 2005, the Singapore Ministry of Defence announced the selection of the F-15SG, a variant of the F-15E, as the fighter of choice for the nation, and twelve examples were ordered. In October 2007, an option for eight additional aircraft on that contract was exercised, as well as a new order for a further four F-15SG, bringing the total to twenty-four. The first F-15SG left the factory on November 3, 2008, and deliveries of all twenty-four were complete by September 2013.

The Strike Eagle began as a private initiative to create an F-15-based aircraft with capabilities comparable to the F-111. The first Strike Eagle was converted from the second F-15, serial number 71-0291. The aircraft is shown here shortly before it made its first flight in Strike Eagle configuration on July 8, 1980, and became the basis of the F-15E. *National Museum of the United States Air Force*

Cathode-ray tubes (CRTs) were a key element of the front and rear cockpits of the F-15E, providing various imaging aids. The CRTs are lit up in this demonstrator, with the weapon systems officer's (WSO's) displays appearing in the foreground, at the bottom of the photo, and the pilot's CRTs and windshield appearing higher up. The CRT displays in the F-15E Strike Eagle offer many benefits to the crew, including improved navigational abilities, more accurate and effective weapons delivery, and overall better systems operations. The pilot has at his disposal redesigned controls, a heads-up display featuring wide field of vision, and three CRTs, which offer multipurpose displays for navigation, systems operations, and weapons delivery. The WSO in the rear seat has an improved ALQ-135 electronic-warfare system with broadband jammer, as well as four CRT displays for weapons selection, radar, and monitoring of enemy tracking systems.

In an overhead view of Strike Eagle 71-0291, white visual-reference markings are around the aerial-refueling receptacle. The dark-gray paint of the camouflage scheme was nearly equal in tone to the dark green, so it is sometimes difficult to distinguish the two colors. Low-visibility black national insignia were applied to the left wing top and to the sides of the fuselage to the front of the engine intakes. This Eagle had been used as a developmental aircraft for the FAST pack conformal fuel tanks. Following its first flight, serial number 71-0291 flew on a demonstration tour in Europe and made an appearance at the Farnborough Air Show in September 1980. The plane was the winning entry in the competition with the F-16XL for the Enhanced Tactical Fighter (ETF) to replace the F-111 and was employed in tests for that purpose at Edwards Air Force Base, California, and Eglin Air Force Base, Florida. This aircraft currently is on display at the Royal Saudi Air Force Museum in Riyadh. *National Museum of the United States Air Force*

Initially, Strike Eagle 71-0291 had the Compass Ghost camouflage scheme. Later, it was repainted in a three-color wraparound camouflage scheme (sometimes disparagingly called "slime green"), comprising dark gray and two shades of green. *National Museum of the United States Air Force*

Strike Eagle 71-0291 is viewed from the rear in a photograph taken in July 1980. "Turkey feathers," long, thin, vanes around the engine exhausts, are present on these engines; they enhanced engine performance but, as high-maintenance items, they often were removed. *National Museum of the United States Air Force*

The prototype Strike Eagle is carrying a load of twenty-six Mk. 82 500-pound bombs on the pylons and on racks attached to the conformal fuel tanks. To support heavy loads such as this, the landing gear and structure of the Strike Eagles would be strengthened. *National Museum of the United States Air Force*

The first production Strike Eagle, F-15E-41-MC, serial number 86-183, is undergoing a test flight. The production F-15Es featured two LANTIRN (low-altitude navigation targeting infrared for night) pods under the engine intakes. These combined terrain-following radar and forward-looking radar to give the pilot and the WSO exceptional navigating and targeting aids. Dummy LANTIRN pods were mounted on this plane. The real pods, which became operational in 1987, consisted of the AAQ-13 navigation pod on the right pylon and the AAQ-14 target pod on the left pylon. *National Museum of the United States Air Force*

The first production F-15E demonstrates its remarkable climbing ability during a test flight over a desert in September 1987. The production F-15Es were painted overall in a dark shade of gray, Gunship Gray (FS36118). The titanium skin around the aft parts of the jet engines remained unpainted. Hardpoints for two air-to-air missiles are on the lower part of each conformal fuel tank. *National Museum of the United States Air Force*

An F-15E Strike Eagle is viewed from directly below during a flight in February 1987. It is carrying three drop tanks as well as the two LANTIRN pods under the engine intakes. Since the LANTIRN pods became operational only during 1987, the two seen here may have been dummies. The longer pod on the left station represents the AAQ-14 target pod, while the shorter pod represents the AAQ-13 navigation pod. *National Museum of the United States Air Force*

McDonnell Douglas F-15E-43-MC Strike Eagle, serial number 87-0173 and manufacturer's number 1038/ E013, assigned to the 389th Fighter Squadron, 366th Fighter Wing, Mountain Home Air Force Base, Idaho, is on display at Travis Air Force Base, California. The colorful vertical tails were painted in honor of the two USAF fighter squadrons based at Mountain Home Air Force Base: the 391st "Bold Tigers" and the 389th "Thunderbolts." *Chris Hughes*

On each side of the forward fuselage is a line depiction of an eagle's head. Red protective covers are over the pitot tube (*lower*) and the angle-of-attack sensor. *Chris Hughes*

A cover to keep out foreign objects is stretched over the left engine intake. It is marked with the plane's serial number and the insignia of the 389th Fighter Squadron. A round sticker on the conformal fuel tank commemorates thirty years of the F-15E Strike Eagle. *Chris Hughes*

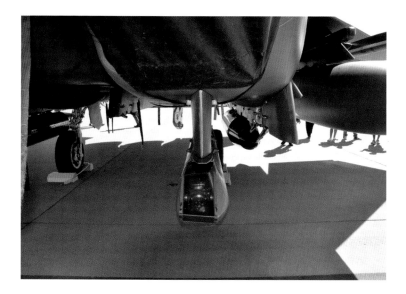

Viewed from the front on the pylon below the left engine intake is a Lockheed Martin Sniper advanced targeting pod (ATP), which provides positive target identification, autonomous tracking of targets, GPS-coordinate generation, and precise weapons guidance from extended standoff ranges. *Chris Hughes*

The Sniper ATP is viewed from the right front. It incorporates a high-definition midwave FLIR (forward-looking infrared), dual-mode laser with a laser-guided bomb designator, visible-light HDTV, a laser spot tracker and marker, and other advanced features. *Chris Hughes*

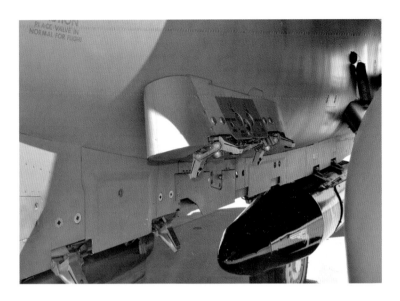

At the center is the forward outboard store station on the left conformal fuel tank. These stations used powder cartridges to eject or drop stores without the stores causing damage to the airframe. *Chris Hughes*

Mounted on the left inboard store station of the F-15E, and seen from the rear, is an MXU-648 travel pod, also called a baggage pod, for transporting the aircrew's personal equipment. These often were converted from napalm-bomb canisters by mounting a door on them. *Chris Hughes*

Marked on the door of the MXU-648 travel pod is "RIDE HARD / SHOOT STRAIGHT / ALWAYS SPEAK THE TRUTH." Also on the pod are renderings of two six-shooters, the crest of the 366th Fighter Wing "Gunfighters," and a "30 Years" Strike Eagle sticker. *Chris Hughes*

In a left-side view of F-15E-43-MC, serial number 87-0173, a 610-gallon external fuel tank is mounted on the wing pylon. Above it, on the outboard launcher rail, is an inert AIM-120 AMRAAM air-to-air missile without the fins installed. *Chris Hughes*

The inert AIM-120 AMRAAM on the left wing pylon is viewed close-up. This missile was used for training purposes; it had an active guidance system, but no means of propulsion or active warhead. *Chris Hughes*

Details of the aft part of the left conformal fuel tank, fuselage, and left vertical tail are displayed. To the left is the aft left outboard store station. The small red object on the bottom center of the store station is the safety handle. *Chris Hughes*

Seen from the rear on the side of the left conformal fuel tank is an air scoop to admit cooling air to the engine compartment. Above it is a red cover over a vent that ejects hot air from the engine compartment. *Chris Hughes*

Covers with the plane's serial number and the 389th Fighter Squadron's insignia are on the jet exhaust nozzles. The outboard side of the left vertical tail features the thunderbolt and tiger symbols of the 389th and 391st Fighter Squadrons. On the inside of the right vertical tail is the "Phantom Gunfighter" symbol of the 366th Fighter Wing. *Chris Hughes*

Details of the right tailplane are shown, including two honeycomb "NO STEP" markings. The positions of the tiger-stripes and thunderbolt motifs on the right vertical tail are reversed from those on the left tail, with the thunderbolt being on the bottom. *Chris Hughes*

In a view featuring the right aileron, the design of the honeycomb "NO STEP" markings is clearly depicted. The black figures along the centerline of the fuselage top spell out "GUNFIGHTERS." *Chris Hughes*

A yellow cover is over the nose of the Sidewinder air-to-air missile on the inboard launcher under the right wing. A red anticollision light is on the leading edge of the wing. On the inboard side of the right vertical fin is a commemoration of the seventy-fifth anniversary of the establishment of Mountain Home Air Force Base in 1943, with the number "75" and the inscription "MHAB 2018 / GUNFIGHTER SKIES," superimposed over an outline map of Idaho. *Chris Hughes*

In a view of the right wing glove and the forward part of the conformal fuel tank, *at the bottom*, on a pylon below the engine-air inlet, is an AN/AAQ-13 LANTIRN (low-altitude navigation and targeting infrared for night) navigational pod. Employing a terrain-following radar and a fixed thermographic camera, LANTIRN provides the capability of high-speed, nap-of-the-earth penetration of enemy territory and precision attack on tactical targets at night and in adverse weather. *Chris Hughes*

US and Israeli ground crews are preparing to tow a USAF F-15E Strike Eagle, *left*, and an Israeli F-15I to hardened shelters during a joint military exercise, Juniper Falcon, at Uvda Air Base, Israel, on May 7, 2017. The F-15I bears serial number 232 on the forward fuselage and has brown, green, and tan over gray camouflage and a large representation of an eagle's head on the left vertical tail.

Three F-15I Ra'ams, including one in the foreground with a satellite-communications dome aft of the canopy, are awaiting clearance to take off on a mission during Exercise Juniper Falcon, at Uvda Air Base, Israel, on May 8, 2017. These Ra'ams bear Israeli air force serial numbers, *from front to rear*, 220, 215, and 252.

The Republic of Korea bought a derivative of the F-15E, the F-15K. Dubbed the Slam Eagle, the F-15K, these were the most-sophisticated versions of the F-15 that the US State Department had permitted to be exported when deliveries began in 2005. *Republic of Korea Ministry of National Defense*

The initial order for 40 F-15K aircraft all had been delivered by the end of 2008; however, in April of that year, the Republic of Korea had ordered a further twenty-one examples. *Republic of Korea Ministry of National Defense*

The F-15K is expected to serve as a total multipurpose fighter, not only securing air superiority but also providing air-to-ground and air-to-sea capabilities. *Republic of Korea Ministry of National Defense*

The F-15K is equipped with the Raytheon (formerly Hughes) APG-63(V)I radar, which is provided with additional sea surface search and ground moving-target-indicator modes. The aircraft is capable of firing the AGM-84D Harpoon and the AGM-84E standoff land attack missile. *Republic of Korea Ministry of National Defense*

On February 28, 2011, a Royal Saudi Air Force F-15S flies over the training lanes, demonstrating their ability to provide air support by dropping flares as simulated bombs during Exercise Friendship Two. The F-15S is based on the F-15E but lacks some of the most sophisticated electronics of the F-15E, which the US government deemed to be too sensitive to export.

The Saudi Arabian F-15SA (F-15 Saudi Advanced) was introduced in 2013. These aircraft are essentially improved versions of the Korean F-15K. Built by Boeing in St. Louis, the eighty-four-unit F-15SA order was augmented by the RSAF decision to upgrade sixty-six of its F-15S aircraft to F-15SA standards, the resultant aircraft being referred to a F-15SR. This F-15SA from the Royal Saudi Air Force Weapons School, at Dhahran, is taking off from Nellis Air Force Base for a Red Flag–Nellis 22-2 sortie, on March 8, 2022.

Air brake extended and tires smoking, an F-15SA assigned to the Royal Saudi Air Force Weapons School, at Dhahran, Saudi Arabia, is touching down at Nellis Air Force Base, Nevada, on March 1, 2022. The plane was slated to participate in the training exercise Red Flag–Nellis 22-2. The angular structure on the fuselage below the cockpit canopy contains a Missile Approach Warning System (MAWS) sensor. On the vertical tail is the code "WS01."

A US Air Force KC-135 Stratotanker is rendezvousing with a Royal Saudi Air Force F-15SA above a desert during a joint multinational training exercise on September 17, 2020. The refueling probe is connected to the receptacle atop the left wing glove. The front end of a targeting pod is below the left engine-air intake.

In December 2005, the Republic of Singapore air force placed an order for twelve derivatives of the F-15E, designated F-15SG. In 2007, a dozen more of the aircraft were ordered, followed by eight more in 2010 and a final eight in 2014. The RSAF personnel responsible for F-15SG operations were trained at Mountain Home Air Force Base, Idaho. Here, a 428th Fighter Squadron crew chief member marshals an F-15SG fighter in front of the Republic of Singapore hangar on May 6, 2009. During a ceremony on May 18, the 366th Fighter Wing, in conjunction with the Republic of Singapore air force, officially activated the 428th Fighter Squadron "Buccaneers" there. Over the life of the program, as many as 2,000 active duty RSAF personnel will have lived and worked on the base. *US Air Force photo by Airman 1st Class Renishia Richardson*

A Republic of Singapore F-15SG Strike Eagle, assigned to the 428th Fighter Squadron, Mountain Home Air Force, Idaho, takes off at Nellis Air Force Base, Nevada, on March 16, 2021, during Red Flag 21-2. Red Flag exercises provide mission commanders, maintenance personnel, ground controllers, and air, space, and cyber operators the opportunity to experience realistic combat scenarios in preparation for future warfare. *US Air National Guard photo by Senior Airman Cameron Lewis*

A Republic of Singapore air force F-15SG taxies off the runway after landing for a deployment on Andersen Air Force Base, Guam, on May 24, 2021. The RSAF has been deploying fighter aircraft to Guam for rotational training since 2017. *US Air Force photo by Senior Airman Michael S. Murphy*

CHAPTER 5

F-15QA and F-15EX Eagle II

An early F-15QA is performing a steep climb. Its skin is a patchwork of various colors; it would be painted in a gray camouflage scheme before delivery.

Beginning with the F-15SA, Boeing introduced numerous upgrades to produce a F-15E-derivative for Qatar, which fittingly was designated the F-15QA (Qatar Advanced) Ababil. The F-15QA is a new-generation Eagle that features fly-by-wire flight controls, an all-glass digital cockpit, and state-of-the-art sensors, radar, and electronic-warfare equipment. Compared to earlier models, the F-15QA has two additional wing hardpoints that allow it to carry up to sixteen AIM-120 AMRAAM air-to-air missiles.

While the F-15QA can operate at altitudes of up to approximately 70,000 feet, it also has a terrain-following radar that allows it to be flown at very low altitudes, with the pilot following cues displayed on a heads-up display.

Approval of the sale, and thus production, was delayed for some time pending State Department and congressional approval. The first F-15QA flew on April 13, 2020.

In 2018, the US Air Force began considering an improved model of the F-15QA to replace the existing fleet of F-15C/D aircraft and augment the new F-35, which has a far lesser weapons payload than the F-15EX.

Dubbed the Eagle II, the F-15EX can carry almost 15 tons of weaponry, much of it held in interior weapons bays, significantly reducing the aircraft's radar signature. While initially both single-seat and two-seat variants were considered, ultimately the Air Force chose to procure only the two-seat model. The Air Force announced plans to procure 144 of the aircraft, the first example of which initially flew on February 2, 2021.

A new F-15QA Ababil fighter for the Qatar Emiri air force, numbered QA500 on the top of the vertical tail, is being officially rolled out at the Boeing factory in St. Louis, Missouri, on August 25, 2021. On the side of the fuselage just below the weapon systems operator's half of the canopy is a small fairing, containing a MAWS sensor.

A Boeing F-15QA (Qatar Advanced) Ababil fighter flying out of MidAmerica St. Louis Airport, adjacent to Scott Air Force Base, Illinois, is approaching a tanker from the 465th Air Refueling Squadron, based at Tinker Air Force Base, Oklahoma, on June 14, 2021.

A curtain has just dropped to unveil the first F-15EX, serial number 20-0001, during the aircraft's naming ceremony at Eglin Air Force Base on April 7, 2021. The "ET" tail code stands for Eglin Test. During testing, the first F-15EX would be flown both by the 40th Flight Test Squadron and the 85th Test and Evaluation Squadron, at Eglin Air Force Base.

More of the first F-15EX is visible in this photo of the plane inside the hangar at the time of the plane's naming ceremony on April 17, 2021. Inert AIM-120C AMRAAM air-to-air missiles have been mounted on the pylons and on the inboard stores stations. The clipped fins are a characteristic of the AIM-120C.

The Boeing F-15EX is a fourth-generation version of the Eagle air-superiority fighter, featuring a modernized cockpit, improved electronic-warfare systems, data-fusion capabilities, improved engines enabling speeds up to Mach 2.5, and other improvements. The first F-15EX is taxiing upon its arrival at Eglin Air Force Base on March 11, 2021. Two easily discerned new features are the identical harmonic balancers on the tops of the vertical fins, and the fairing on the fuselage below the canopy. An identical fairing is also on the opposite side of the fuselage: evidently these were installed to accommodate the future installation of MAWS sensors.

The number one F-15EX Eagle II, under assignment to the 53rd Wing, Eglin Air Force Base, Florida, is taxiing to the runway in preparation for taking off from Nellis Air Force Base, Nevada, on October 21, 2021. This plane was at Nellis to conduct integrated test and evaluation. The insignia of the 40th Flight Test Squadron is on the front end of the conformal fuel tank. A nomenclature-and-serial-number stencil is on the side of the tilted-down engine-air intake: it identifies the plane as "F-15EX-87-MC SERIAL NUMBER 20-0001A."

The second F-15EX Eagle II, serial number 20-0002, banks hard during its first test flight out of Eglin Air Force Base, on April 26, 2021, prior to departing for Northern Edge '21, an operational-testing exercise in Alaska, in May 2021. This F-15EX was delivered to the 85th Test and Evaluation Squadron a few days earlier. The previously seen fairing below the right side of the canopy has an identical mate on the left side, visible here.

The second F-15EX Eagle II, seen during its initial test flight from Eglin, bears on its left vertical tail an "OT" tail code, markings for the 53rd Wing, and the tail number 20002.

On the inboard launcher of the wing pylon of the second F-15EX is an ACMI (air-combat maneuvering instrumentation) pod, which serves as a data link to enable personnel on the ground to monitor the aircraft's instruments and fire-control system during simulated combat flights.

During a hard bank during the initial test flight on April 26, 2021, the second F-15EX displays its underside. A major change that came with the adoption of the F110-GE-129 engines is the reinstatement of the long-discontinued turkey feathers on the engine exhaust nozzles. Not easily discerned are attachment points for two additional pylons, outboard of the existing pylons.

The first two F-15EX Eagle II aircraft, 20-0001 (*in the background*) and 20-0002 (*in the foreground*), serving with the 40th Flight Test Squadron, are ready for preflight inspection prior to an integrated test and evaluation flight from Nellis Air Force Base, Nevada, on October 21, 2021. Both planes have a Sniper advanced targeting pod (ATP) mounted under the left engine-air intake and, apparently, a LANTIRN pod under the right intake.

A ground crewman assists the pilot of an F-15A that has arrived at Luke Air Force Base, Arizona, in May 1974. This was several months before the first operational F-15 was delivered to Luke, in November 1974. Two more F-15As are in the background. *National Archives*

As of early 2022, the F-15 family of aircraft maintains the enviable record of having never lost an air-to-air engagement, yet having racked up over 100 victories. Further, this has been accomplished while having lost shockingly few aircraft to ground-to-air missiles, despite the type having been in use for almost fifty years in the hands of pilots around the world.

The Eagle scored its first kill in 1979 in the hands of Israeli pilot Moshe Melnik. From 1979 through 1981, Israel claimed thirteen Syrian MiG-21s and two Syrian MiG-25s downed, with a further forty-one Syrian aircraft shot down during the 1982 Lebanon War.

Saudi Arabia reported its Eagles had downed two Iranian air force F-4 Phantom IIs in 1984.

US Air Force Eagle victories began to accrue during the First Gulf War, where F-15s accounted for thirty-six of the thirty-nine USAF aerial wins during the war. It is also during that war that the USAF F-15Es drew their first blood, hunting at night for SCUD missile launchers, unfortunately losing two of their number to antiaircraft fire.

An F-15A, USAF serial number 72-0115, poses next to one of its ancestors, a Spad XIII fighter from World War I, at Lockbourne Air Force Base, Ohio, on the occasion of that base's renaming to Rickenbacker Air Force Base, May 17, 1974. *National Archives*

"Streak Eagle," preproduction F-15A, serial number 72-0119, was diverted from the test program to serve as a vehicle for attempting a new time-to-climb record in 1975. This plane served in that role in an unpainted state to reduce its weight; "Streak Eagle" art was on the nose. *National Museum of the United States Air Force*

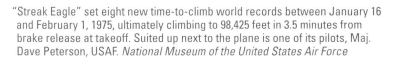

"Streak Eagle" set eight new time-to-climb world records between January 16 and February 1, 1975, ultimately climbing to 98,425 feet in 3.5 minutes from brake release at takeoff. Suited up next to the plane is one of its pilots, Maj. Dave Peterson, USAF. *National Museum of the United States Air Force*

"Streak Eagle" flies over downtown St. Louis, Missouri. The patchy, multicolored appearance of the plane was owing to the unpainted mix of composites and metals used on the aircraft. "USAF" over "20119" was marked in black on the vertical tail. *National Museum of the United States Air Force*

The air intake of "Streak Eagle" is canted downward in this shot, revealing a wedge-shaped area of metal skin that is lighter than the surrounding surfaces. Under the canopy to the rear of the pilot's seat is a white object that was unique to the "Streak Eagle": a large VHF antenna. *National Museum of the United States Air Force*

"Streak Eagle" was equipped with an air-data boom with alpha and beta vanes (alpha vanes register angle of attack, while beta vanes detect aircraft angle of sideslip). By not painting "Streak Eagle," the plane was spared 50 pounds of extra weight. Equipment not essential to the mission was removed, such as the gun and ammunition, radar and fire-control gear, flap and speed-brake actuators, and nonessential communications devices. *National Museum of the United States Air Force*

By the time this photograph of "Streak Eagle" was taken, a large insignia had been applied to the vertical tail. Its motto read "Aquila Maxima," Latin for "Greatest Eagle." Visible on the insignia is an eagle's head with a red, white, and blue streamer behind it. *National Museum of the United States Air Force*

The "Aquila Maxima" insignia on the left vertical tail of the "Streak Eagle" is partially visible. Following the record-setting flights, "Streak Eagle" was painted to protect it from corrosion. As of 2022, the aircraft is in storage at the National Museum of the United States Air Force, at Wright-Patterson Air Force Base. *National Museum of the United States Air Force*

F-15A-6-MC, serial number 72-117, was one of the Category 2 preproduction Eagles, and it is seen in its original Air Superiority Blue camouflage, banking right over Locks & Dam 27 near St. Louis. This was one of the F-15As transferred to the Israeli defense forces / air force. *National Archives*

On March 20, 1976, F-15A-10-MC, serial number 74-083, the first Eagle to be delivered to the 1st Tactical Fighter Wing, is parked next to a General Dynamics F-111. The nickname "Peninsula Patriot" is written in small, old-fashioned lettering aft of the radome. *National Museum of the United States Air Force*

Photographed on March 20, 1976, McDonnell Douglas F-15B-10-MC, USAF serial number 74-137, bears the "FF" tail code of the 1st Tactical Fighter Wing. The last three digits of the serial number, 137, are stenciled on the fuselage just aft of the radome. *National Museum of the United States Air Force*

F-15A-9-MC, serial number 73-100, was not yet assigned unit markings when this photo was taken. This was the first F-15 to leave the factory painted in the Compass Ghost camouflage, which featured patterns of Dark Ghost Gray (FS36320) over Light Ghost Gray (FS36375). *National Archives*

Carrying a 610-gallon auxiliary fuel tank on the centerline, F-15A-15-MC, serial number 76-0039, of the 36th Tactical Fighter Wing, stationed at Bitburg Air Base, Federal Republic of Germany, visits RAF Alconbury, England, for aggressor training exercises in October 1977. *National Museum of the United States Air Force*

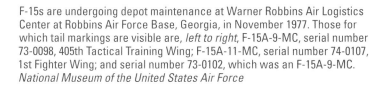

F-15s are undergoing depot maintenance at Warner Robbins Air Logistics Center at Robbins Air Force Base, Georgia, in November 1977. Those for which tail markings are visible are, *left to right*, F-15A-9-MC, serial number 73-0098, 405th Tactical Training Wing; F-15A-11-MC, serial number 74-0107, 1st Fighter Wing; and serial number 73-0102, which was an F-15A-9-MC. *National Museum of the United States Air Force*

On March 20, 1978, F-15B-16-MC, serial number 76-0135, of the 7th Tactical Fighter Squadron, 49th Tactical Fighter Wing, is parked on a hardstand at Holloman Air Force Base, New Mexico. The 49th TFW's original insignia is on the engine intake trunk. *National Museum of the United States Air Force*

Four of the US Air Force's fighter jets are lined up during a tactical-fighter training mission out of Luke Air Force Base on August 1, 1979. At the top is F-15A-16-MC, serial number 76-0078, of the 550th Tactical Training Squadron, 58th Tactical Training Wing. Below the F-15A are an F-4C Phantom II, an F-104 Starfighter, and an F-5E Tiger II.

McDonnell Douglas F-15A-9-MC Eagle, serial number 73-0103, was painted in Air Superiority Blue, with red and white stripes painted on the wings and forward fuselage for high visibility, while serving with the 461st Tactical Fighter Training Squadron, 405th Tactical Fighter Training Wing, at Luke Air Force Base, Arizona, in the last half of the 1970s.

Two 49th Fighter Wing F-15s are sitting on a hardstand awash with recent rainwater at Holloman Air Force Base, New Mexico, in May 1980. Both Eagles have red bands on the upper parts of their vertical tails, indicating they belonged to the 9th Fighter Squadron. *National Museum of the United States Air Force*

In a companion view to the preceding photo, two of the 9th Fighter Squadron's F-15A-18-MCs, serial numbers 77-0069, *left*, and 77-0073, *right*, prepare to taxi out for a mission at Holloman Air Force Base, New Mexico, on May 1, 1980.

Two F-15 Eagles of the 433rd Fighter Weapons Squadron have completed a training mission and are homeward bound to Nellis Air Force Base, Nevada, on May 1, 1980. An AIM-9L Sidewinder air-to-air missile is mounted a launching rail on the outboard side of the left pylon on each aircraft. On the inboard side of the left pylons are combat training-system pods, apparently of the P3 or P4 type produced by Cubic Corp.

Ground crewmen perform maintenance on an F-15 Eagle assigned to the 18th Tactical Fighter Wing during Exercise Pacific Consort on August 19, 1980. Although a retractable crew ladder was built into the F-15s' fuselages, the detachable ladder seen here was always the preferred means of accessing the cockpit. In the foreground is one of the various ground-support equipment carts that were essential to maintaining the Air Force's jets.

Based at Langley Air Force Base, Virginia, F-15A-17-MC, serial number 76-0100, served with the 48th Fighter Interceptor Squadron in the 1980s. This squadron was equipped with F-15As from 1982 to 1991, during which year the squadron was inactivated. The insignia of the 48th FIS is on the side of the engine intake.

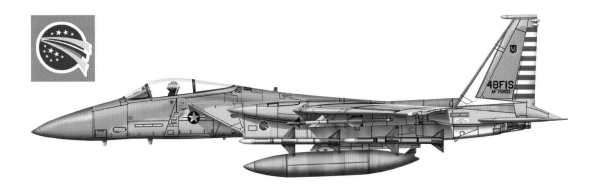

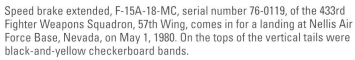

Speed brake extended, F-15A-18-MC, serial number 76-0119, of the 433rd Fighter Weapons Squadron, 57th Wing, comes in for a landing at Nellis Air Force Base, Nevada, on May 1, 1980. On the tops of the vertical tails were black-and-yellow checkerboard bands.

In the foreground is F-15B-19-MC, serial number 77-0157; in the background are F-15A-19-MC, serial number 77-0089, and F-15A-18-MC, serial number 77-0082. The "EG" code and blue tail stripes mark these planes as part of the 58th Fighter Squadron, 33rd Fighter Wing, Eglin Air Force Base.

AIM-9 Sidewinder air-to-air missiles on launcher racks on the right-wing pylon of an F-15A are viewed from the front. Yellow safety caps are fitted over the seeker heads of the missiles, and "REMOVE BEFORE FLIGHT" tags are attached to safety pins.

A pilot of the 18th Tactical Fighter Wing is standing up in the cockpit of an F-15 Eagle prior to a mission during Exercise Pacific Consort on August 19, 1980. On the access door of the radar equipment bay is a panel with a black outline in which the armament for the current mission was written with an erasable marker. Visible inside the bay is the array of black boxes associated with the APG-63 pulse-Doppler radar system.

AIM-7F Sparrow air-to-air missiles are mounted on the left side of an F-15 Eagle alert aircraft parked on the flight line at Osan Air Base, Republic of Korea, on October 1, 1980. A close-up view is available of the tail fins and the exhaust of the one in the foreground.

A parked F-15 Eagle at an unidentified air base is armed with four AIM-9 Sidewinder air-to-air missiles on June 12, 1981. Aft of the cockpit is the grille for the cockpit air conditioner. The dark areas on the tops of the engine intakes are bleed-air ducts. On the right glove alongside the right engine intake, the two dark squares are ventilation grilles for the M61 20 mm gun bay; the forward one is an air intake, and the rear one is an air outlet.

Maintenance personnel hook a tow bar to the nose gear of an F-15 Eagle aircraft at Osan Air Base on October 1, 1980. Two light assemblies are on the nose-gear strut: the upper, smaller one is a taxi light. The larger one is the landing light. Red covers are positioned over the engine intakes. Stenciled on them are "12 AMB" and "THINK FOD," a reference to foreign-object damage and a reminder to constantly check the intakes for any debris, no matter how small, which could cause serious damage to the engines.

An F-15 banks right out of formation with F-15C-24-MC USAF serial number 79-0019 during a flight in 1981. The "CR" tail code on the closer plane indicates it was assigned to the 32nd Fighter Squadron. The tail band is orange outlined in green. *National Museum of the United States Air Force*

On a cold, snowy day at Bitburg Air Base, Federal Republic of Germany, on January 1, 1982, an F-15 Eagle is taxiing along the flight line. The aircraft is carrying a 610-gallon centerline auxiliary fuel tank. On the tail is the "CR" code of the 36th Fighter Wing.

Two F-15s of the 33rd Tactical Fighter Wing, based at Eglin Air Force Base, Florida, are viewed from above during a flight over the water on April 28, 1982. These planes were participating in "Ocean Venture," joint-services maritime war games. *National Museum of the United States Air Force*

An F-15 Eagle is undergoing a check of its jet engines at the Engine Test Cell, Bitburg Air Base, Federal Republic of Germany, on October 22, 1981. Steam is rising from the cell, caused by water being injected into the hot exhaust gases of the engines.

The first F-15C, USAF serial number 78-0468, is viewed from below during store-separation testing of the Mk. 82 low-drag general-purpose (LDGP) bombs loaded on pylons attached to the conformal fuel tanks, during August 1983. *National Museum of the United States Air Force*

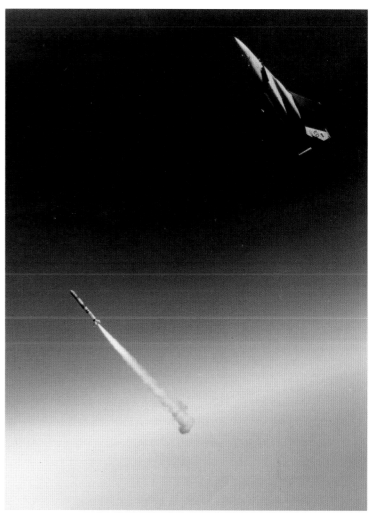

An important tactic in modern warfare would be to knock out enemy reconnaissance and communications satellites. To this end, ASAT missiles were developed. An F-15 is seen test-firing one of them near Edwards Air Force Base in September 1985. *National Museum of the United States Air Force*

The LTV Aerospace ASM-135 ASAT (antisatellite missile) was designed to be launched by F-15As to knock out enemy satellites. Here, an ASAT is on a bomb-lift truck, with F-15A-18-MC, serial number 77-0084, parked in the background, on August 1, 1982. *National Archives*

An F-15C-28-MC, USAF serial number 80-0032, with the "FF" tail code of the 1st Fighter Wing, is undergoing an engine change at a base at Khartoum, Sudan, during Arid Farmer, a deployment made in response to Libyan activities in Chad, on August 15, 1983.

Members of the 12th Aircraft Maintenance Unit install a new Pratt & Whitney F100-PW-100 engine in F-15D-22-MC, serial number 78-0566, of the 12th Fighter Squadron, 18th Fighter Wing, during Exercise Cope North 85-1, on November 8, 1984, at Chitose Air Base, Japan.

In a photo taken shortly after the preceding one, technicians from the 12th Aircraft Maintenance Unit have maneuvered a new Pratt & Whitney F100-PW-100 engine partway into the left engine bay of an F-15D during Exercise COPE NORTH 85-1.

The lead F-15 of the 1st Tactical Fighter Wing, Langley Air Force Base, Virginia, is seen during a flight on June 15, 1983. "1ST TFW," the tail code "FF," and the Tactical Air Command insignia are on the tail. This Eagle is armed with two AIM-9 Sidewinder missiles on the wing pylon and four fuselage-mounted AIM-7 Sparrow missiles. On the engine-intake trunk are the insignias of the three fighter squadrons in the 1st TFW: the 27th TFS, 71st TFS, and 94th TFS.

On March 19, 1986, McDonnell Douglas F-15C-21-MC, serial number 78-0489, piloted by Capt. Patrick E. Duffy of the 67th Tactical Fighter Squadron, 18th Tactical Fighter Wing, escorts a Soviet Tupelov TU-95 Bear bomber that had approached the US Fleet during Team Spirit 86, a joint US–South Korean military exercise. The squadron flew numerous escort sorties against intruding Soviet aircraft during the exercise. *National Museum of the United States Air Force*

F-15A-18-MC, serial number 77-067, assigned to the 8th Tactical Fighter Squadron, 49th Tactical Fighter Wing, is parked at Naval Air Station Whidbey Island in the state of Washington in August 1986. The plane was there to present a flight demonstration. *National Museum of the United States Air Force*

F-15A-17-MC, serial number 76-0086, armed with an ASM-135 ASAT missile, is banking to the left over Vandenberg Air Force Base Tracking Station in early 1985. On the vertical tail is an insignia with the legend "ASAT EAGLE" over "SATELLITE KILLER." *National Museum of the United States Air Force*

Two F-15A-11-MCs, USAF serial numbers 74-105 and 74-099, serving with the 43rd Tactical Fighter Squadron out of Elmendorf Air Force Base, Anchorage, Alaska, fly in formation during a mission in 1986. They are armed with AIM-7 and AIM-9 missiles. *National Museum of the United States Air Force*

On March 19, 1987, the first production Strike Eagle, F-15E-41-MC, serial number 86-183, *foreground*, and F-15B-20-MC, serial number 77-0166, fly together over Edwards Air Force Base, California. The F-15B has the "ED" tail code of the Air Force Flight Test Center at Edwards AFB. *National Museum of the United States Air Force*

Ground crewmen use a winch and cable to pull a 58th Tactical Fighter Squadron F-15 into its hangar during Exercise Cornet Phaser, a NATO rapid-deployment exercise, at a base at Lahr, Federal Republic of Germany, on October 5, 1987.

F-15C-40-MC, serial number 85-0112, of the 33rd Tactical Fighter Wing, fires an AIM-7 Sparrow missile at a target on the Gulf Range as part of Combat Archer, the Weapon System Evaluation program at Tyndall Air Force Base, Florida, on January 1, 1988.

Its radome and electronics access doors swung open, an F-15 Eagle aircraft is undergoing servicing on a flight line at an unidentified airfield on November 30, 1988. A red cover is fitted over the radar antenna, to protect its delicate and sensitive parts while not in use.

An F-15 is inverted on a pedestal at the Rome Air Development Center's Irish Hill test site near Rome, New York, in July 1986. This was a means of quickly evaluating the effectiveness of a plane's antennas at different angles and with various underwing stores.

A photographer in a KC-10A tanker took this photo of an F-15E Strike Eagle of the 336th Tactical Fighter Squadron breaking away after being refueled on September 12, 1989. Visible under the right inlet is the AAQ-13 navigation pod of the LANTIRN system. *National Museum of the United States Air Force*

A KC-10 Extender tanker is refueling an F-15E Strike Eagle assigned to the 336th Tactical Fighter Squadron somewhere high over North Carolina on March 27, 1989. Prior to refueling, the door of the refueling receptacle, which was hinged on the front, swung downward into the recess to the front of the receptacle. The door swung back up when refueling was complete. *National Museum of the United States Air Force*

Two F-15E Strike Eagles of the 336th Tactical Fighter Squadron fly in formation in September 1989. The plane in the foreground was crewed by Lieutenant Colonels M. Decuir and John Delouey, and the one in the background by Capts. Mark Mouw and Gregory Torba. *National Museum of the United States Air Force*

An F-15C of the 33rd Tactical Fighter Wing, based at Eglin Air Force Base, Florida, banks left during an October 16, 1989, flight. It is carrying two AIM-9 Sidewinder missiles on each of the two wing pylons, and four AIM-120 advanced medium-range air-to-air missiles (AMRAAMs) on the fuselage missile stations. A 610-gallon fuel tank is on the centerline. *National Museum of the United States Air Force*

An F-15 Eagle from the 49th Tactical Fighter Wing, Holloman AFB, New Mexico, approaches the runway for a landing on or around January 1, 1990. The blue bands on the vertical tail indicate that this plane was serving with the 7th Tactical Fighter Squadron.

Two crewmen from the 58th Operational Support Squadron, 58th Fighter Wing, make last-minute checks of and arm the practice bombs on the pylons of an F-15E Strike Eagle of the 461st Fighter Squadron at Luke Air Force Base, Arizona, on February 1, 1993. *National Museum of the United States Air Force*

NASA operated this HIDEC (highly integrated digital electronic control) F-15, seen here while making a landing after a flight out of NASA's Dryden Flight Research Center, Edwards, California, in 1993. Originally, this plane was F-15A, USAF serial number 71-0287. It carried NASA aircraft number 835 on the tail. One of the projects it was employed in was the development of a computer-assisted engine-control system that allows a plane to land using only engine power if its control surfaces are disabled.

On April 12, 1993, F-15C-35-MC, serial number 84-0019, of the 53rd Fighter Squadron taxis at Aviano Air Base, Italy, before departing on Operation Deny Flight: a mission to enforce a United Nations–sanctioned no-fly zone in Bosnia and Herzegovina. *National Museum of the United States Air Force*

F-15C-37-MC, serial number 84-0005, of the 53rd Fighter Squadron is being serviced at Aviano Air Base, Italy, during Operation Deny Flight on April 16, 1993. On the left pylon is the pilot's travel pod, decorated with red and yellow stripes, for carrying his personal gear. *National Museum of the United States Air Force*

In June 1994, F-15C-37-MC, serial number 84-0014, assigned to the 53rd Fighter Squadron, 36th Fighter Wing, has landed at Aviano Air Base, Italy, for maintenance following a combat mission over Bosnia to enforce the no-fly zone. The 53rd FS's yellow band is at the top of the tail. *National Museum of the United States Air Force*

A stylized Eagle is on the tail of this F-15A-17-MC, serial number 76-0106, photographed in May 1993 while flying a surveillance mission against drug runners in Panama. This plane was part of Air Forces Panama, the US Air Force command tasked with the defense of the Panama Canal, and specifically the plane was assigned to Coronet Night Hawk, an all-Guard mission that employed both F-15s and F-16s on a twenty-four-hour-alert basis. *National Museum of the United States Air Force*

The Israeli air force operated this F-15C, tail number 840. It is shown during its service with 106 Squadron. During its career, this Eagle was credited with shooting down six Syrian planes; six kill markings are on the fuselage forward of the windscreen, below which is repeated the tail number, 840. The inscription on the radome translates to "Skyblazer."

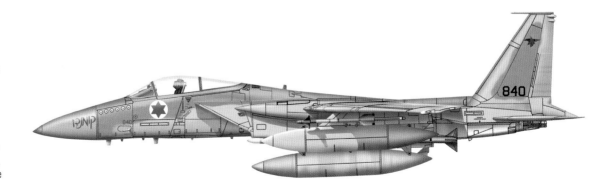

The first preproduction TF-15A (F-15B), serial number 71-0290, was converted to the colorfully painted F-15 STOL/MTD (short takeoff and landing / maneuver technology demonstrator) while on loan to NASA in the 1980s. When this photo was taken around early 1996, the plane was being used as the F-15 ACTIVE (Advanced Control Technology for Integrated Vehicles), a joint project of NASA, the US Air Force, McDonnell Douglas Aerospace, and Pratt & Whitney, from 1993 to 1999. The plane was powered by Pratt & Whitney F100-PW-229 engines modified with multidirectional thrust-vectoring nozzles. On April 24, 1996, this aircraft completed its first supersonic yaw-vectoring flight at Dryden Flight Research Center, Edwards, California.

F-15D-40-MC, serial number 85-0134, of the 33rd Fighter Wing prepares to taxi to the runway at Roosevelt Roads Naval Air Station, Puerto Rico, around September 1, 1994. It was part of a flight of twenty-four F-15s on a return trip to their home base at Eglin Air Force Base, Florida.

A new Pratt & Whitney F100-PW-220E turbofan engine for an F-15 Eagle, a power plant designed to reduce maintenance hours, is being operated in the test-cell hush house (a chamber used to reduce noise pollution) at Kadena Air Base, Japan, on May 11, 1998.

A USAF maintenance technician is standing inside the left engine bay of an F-15 Eagle during a major overhaul of the aircraft around 1999, shining a red flashlight on the interior of the compartment while he inspects it. Another maintenance tech, crouching at the lower left of the photo, notes any discrepancies in the aircraft-maintenance forms.

On November 6, 2001, F-15A-19-MC, serial number 77-0102, of the 102nd Fighter Wing, Massachusetts Air National Guard, flies a combat air patrol (CAP) mission over New York City during Operation Noble Eagle, a homeland security operation in the wake of 9/11.

F-15A-19-MC, serial number 77-0118, with "SL" markings for the 131st Fighter Wing, prepares to take off from Prince Sultan Air Base, Saudi Arabia, during Operation Southern Watch on October 24, 2000. This operation was to enforce a mandated no-fly/no-drive zone in southern Iraq. *National Archives*

An F-15E of the 332nd Air Expeditionary Group is departing on a bombing mission to Afghanistan on November 7, 2001. It is armed with a GBU-15 electro-optic guided bomb under the right wing, its associated AN-AXQ-14 data link pod under the fuselage centerline, and a GBU-12 Paveway II laser-guided bomb on the right CFT.

In May 2002, an F-15A-20-MC, USAF serial number 77-0134, assigned to the 122nd Fighter Squadron, Louisiana Air National Guard, based at New Orleans, cruises over Cape San Blas, Florida. The plane and crew had just completed a Combat Archer training mission. Combat Archer, also known as the Air-to-Air Weapons-Evaluation Program, was hosted by the 83rd Fighter Weapons Squadron at Tyndall Air Force Base, Florida. The tail band is purple, yellow, and green, with five fleur-de-lis on the yellow part; "Louisiana" is written above the band. The "JZ" tail code stands for, of course, "Jazz." *National Museum of the United States Air Force*

NASA acquired the second F-15B (serial number 71-0290), redesignating it NF-15B, tail number 837, and converting it to an Intelligent Flight Control System (IFCS) research test bed. NASA fitted the plane with canards and two pitch-yaw balance-beam nozzles.

McDonnell Douglas F-15E-58-MC Strike Eagle, USAF serial number 96-0205, serving with 492nd Fighter Squadron, 48th Fighter Wing, based at RAF Lakenheath, England, catches a Mobile Aircraft Arresting System (MAAS) wire during a deployment to Ṭallîl Air Base, near an-Nâṣirîyah, in southern Iraq, in support of Operation Iraqi Freedom on May 25, 2004. The tail code is LN, and the tail bands are blue with white borders.

Ground crewmen remove the MAAS cable from the arrestor hook of the same F-15E depicted in the preceding photo, after landing at Ṭallîl Air Base. A tow bar is secured to the nose landing gear, to enable a tractor to pull the aircraft to its parking area.

This long view of the same F-15E seen in the two preceding photos shows more of the MAAS cable, which is still attached to the arrestor hook. The rear ends of the cable are attached to tires, which in turn are fastened to thick webbing straps.

F-15C-23-MCs of the 44th Fighter Squadron, 18th Fighter Wing, based at Kadena Air Base, Japan, fly in formation over Okinawa on May 4, 2004. On the pylons are AIM-120 AMRAAMs and Combat Training System / Tactical Combat Training System pods. Activated on January 1, 1944, the 44th Fighter Squadron served with distinction in the South Pacific and Southwest Pacific in World War II and flew missions against North Vietnam from bases in Thailand during the Vietnam War. The 44th Fighter Squadron was based at Kadena Air Base from March 1971 onward, with occasional deployments to a variety of bases in the Western Pacific. The squadron first acquired the F-15Cs in February 1980, flying that model of the Eagle for many years thereafter.

This extreme close-up view of the aerial refueling of an F-15E Strike Eagle of the 335th Fighter Squadron, 4th Fighter Wing, based at Seymour Johnson Air Force Base, North Carolina, was taken by a photographer in a KC-10A Extender cargo/tanker of the 763rd Expeditionary Air Refueling Squadron, Al Dhafra Air Base, United Arab Emirates, during a combat mission in support of Operation Iraqi Freedom on August 16, 2004. The Strike Eagle is armed with AIM-120A AMRAAMs on the outboard side of the pylons, and AIM-9M Sidewinders on the inboard sides of the pylons. Four GBU-12 500-pound bombs are visible under the CFTs, and the front end of an AN/AAQ-28(V) targeting pod can be seen under the left engine intake.

Two Israeli defense forces / air force F-15I Eagles practice air-defense maneuvers during a training mission over the Nevada Test and Training Ranges at Nellis Air Force Base, Nevada, during Exercise Red Flag in 2004. Exercise Red Flag is a realistic combat-training exercise in which the air forces of the United States and its allies hone their crafts. The IDF/AF became interested in acquiring the F-15 Eagle by 1974, when its pilots tested the TF-15A. The following year, Israel submitted an order for twenty-five F-15As. Deliveries of F-15s to Israel commenced in December 1976. Israeli F-15s first drew blood in 1979, and subsequently they have been credited with shooting down many Syrian fighter planes, and they have conducted numerous long-range missions, such as the raid on Palestine Liberation Organization headquarters in Tunis, Tunisia, on October 1, 1985.

Using a special ammo cart, armorers of the 123rd Fighter Squadron, 142nd Fighter Wing, Oregon National Guard, load 20 mm ammunition into an F-15 Eagle during the William Tell 2004 gunnery competition at Tyndall Air Force Base, Florida, on November 10, 2004.

During the Hawaii Air National Guard Operational Readiness Exercise at Hickam Air Force Base, Hawaii, in February 2004, an aircraft maintainer wearing mission-oriented protective posture level 4 (MOPP-4) gear checks the left rudder of F-15A-18-MC, USAF serial number 76-0120. This Eagle was assigned to the 154th Wing, based at Hickam Air Force Base. A clear view is available of, *from top to bottom on the trailing edge of the left tail*, the AN/ALQ-128 electronic-warfare warning-system antenna, the AN/ALR-56 radar-warning receiver antenna, and the red anticollision light. At the top of the right tail is a spike-shaped harmonic balancer, and on the rear of that tail are an AN/ALR-56 antenna and red anticollision light.

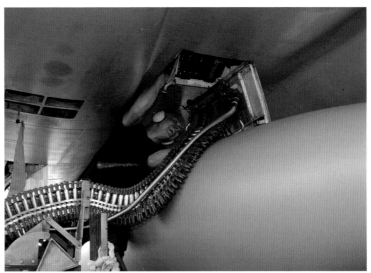

SSgt. Kevin Skaggs of the 95th Air Maintenance Unit wrestles a flex chute into place, to send 940 rounds of 20 mm training projectiles into an F-15 Eagle during a flight-line loading competition at William Tell 2004, Tyndall Air Force Base, on November 12, 2004.

An F-15E-47-MC, USAF serial number 89-0487, has caught an arrestor wire during a landing at an unidentified desert air base. This plane has markings on the tail for the 335th Fighter Squadron, 4th Fighter Wing; at the top of the tail is a green band edged in white.

McDonnell Douglas F-15C-35-MC, serial number 83-0027, from the 27th Tactical Fighter Squadron flies past the Pyramids of Giza during a deployment to the Middle East. The squadron insignia, featuring an eagle over a red disk on a yellow circular background, is on the engine intake. *National Archives*

The tanker refueling this F-15E Strike Eagle during April 2006 has cast a shadow across the cockpit area. Three AIM-120 AMRAAMs are visible on the launcher racks. The fronts of two laser-guided bombs can be seen under the right conformal fuel tank.

F-15E-42-MC, serial number 86-0189, of the 335th Fighter Squadron (indicated by the green bands at the tops of the vertical tails), 4th Fighter Wing, is parked at an unidentified base. The insignia of the 4th Fighter Wing is on the front of the CFT.

Two F-15 Eagles with "aggressor" camouflage schemes accompany a USAF F-22 Raptor fighter during a training mission over Nevada on April 24, 2008. The Eagles were assigned to the 65th Aggressor Squadron at Nellis Air Force Base. In the tan-and-brown camouflage in the foreground is F-15D-39-MC, serial number 85-0129, while the blue-on-blue plane appears to be F-15C-27-MC, serial number 80-0018.

Photographed in January 2009, this modified F-15B, NASA tail number 836, has served as a supersonic research test bed and mission-support aircraft for NASA's Armstrong Flight Research Center in Edwards, California, since the early 1990s.

NASA's canard-equipped NF-15B research plane, tail number 837, takes off from Edwards Air Force Base on its last flight on January 30, 2009. The canards of the NF-15B had a span of 26.5 feet, compared with the plane's wingspan of 42.8 feet.

NASA Dryden's NF-15B, tail number 837, is parked on a hardstand, canards tilted down, during a preflight control check prior to a Lancets (Lift and Nozzle Change Effects on Tail Shock project) flight, part of a project to design quieter supersonic aircraft.

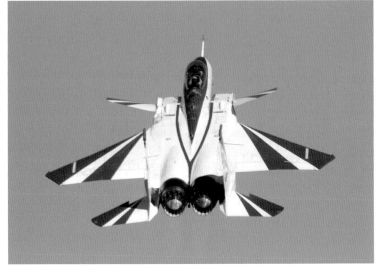

Afterburners glowing, NASA's NF-15B soars from the runway at Edwards Air Force Base on its final flight. Test pilot Jim Smolka was at the controls. The first two-seat F-15, it had a useful career as a test plane for McDonnell Douglas, the Air Force, and NASA.

F-15C-23-MC, serial number 78-0528, of the 65th Aggressor Squadron flies over Nevada on May 17, 2012. This plane and others in its squadron flew in support of and engaged in simulated dogfights against members of the Air Force Weapons School at Nellis, a five-and-a-half-month training course that provides advanced training in weapons and tactics employment.

Speed brake extended, F-15E-47-MC, USAF serial number 89-0487, of the 4th Fighter Wing lands at Bagram Air Field, Afghanistan, after racking up its 10,000th flight hour, on January 14, 2012. This was the first F-15E to attain 10,000 hours of flying time.

F-15D-27-MC, serial number 80-0054, of the 57th Fighter Wing at Nellis Air Force Base, Nevada, has a distinguished passenger aboard. The crew placard, decorated with an eagle head, alongside the cockpit lists pilot Maj. Julius Romasanta and Gen. Chuck Yeager.

F-15E, serial number 88-1708, from the 4th Fighter Wing, permanently based at Seymour Johnson Air Force Base, North Carolina, has just taken off on a mission from Bagram Air Field, Afghanistan, on December 15, 2011. *TSgt. Matt Hecht / US Air National Guard*

McDonnell Douglas F-15D-39-MC Eagle, serial number 85-0129, is parked on a ramp at Great Falls Air National Guard Base, in Montana, on September 12, 2012. The Eagle was painted in a tan-and-brown desert camouflage with a gray radome and bears on the inboard side of the right vertical tail the "Vigilantes" nickname of the 186th Fighter Squadron, Montana Air National Guard. On the left vertical fin are, *near the top*, the inscription "Montana" between two horizontal lines, and, *center*, a representation of a bison skull.

A Japan Air Self-Defense Force (JASDF) F-15 Eagle, tail number 82-8965, takes off from Eileson Air Force Base, Alaska, during Red Flag-Alaska 13-3 on August 9, 2013. An insignia constituting a yellow eagle inside a black circular background is on the vertical tail.

The same JASDF F-15 Eagle shown in the preceding photo is viewed from a slightly different perspective during takeoff from Eileson Air Force Base. The Japanese sent six aircraft and more than 150 airmen to participate in Red Flag-Alaska 13-3.

An F-15E Strike Eagle of the 391st Fighter Squadron is releasing defensive flares during a close-air-support mission during exercise Mountain Roundup 2013, at Saylor Creek bombing range near Mountain Home Air Force Base, Idaho, on October 16, 2013.

One of the last three F-15 Eagle fighter aircraft assigned to the 120th Fighter Wing takes off from the Great Falls International Airport (Montana) on October 24, 2013. Those Eagles were transferred to the California Air National Guard on that date.

On November 26, 2013, an Israeli defense forces / air force F-15D takes off from Uvda Air Force Base, Israel, during Blue Flag: a multinational aerial-warfare exercise hosted by Israel to foster greater coordination among the air forces of the US, Israel, Greece, and Italy.

An F-15C-35-MC, serial number 84-0014, assigned to Col. Clay Garrison but piloted by Col. John York, 144th Fighter Wing operations group commander, flies over central California on November 7, 2013. The wing was transitioning to the F-15 from the F-16.

Personnel of the 48th Aircraft Maintenance Squadron perform postflight servicing on an F-15E Strike Eagle in preparation for the Blue Flag exercise at Uvda Air Force Base, Israel, on November 19, 2013. The insignia of the 492nd Fighter Squadron is on the CFT.

A column of F-15E Strike Eagles of the 492nd Fighter Squadron, based at Royal Air Force Lakenheath, taxis at Uvda Air Force Base, Israel, after a simulated combat mission during the Blue Flag exercise on November 26, 2013.

An F-15E Strike Eagle takes off from Uvda Air Force Base, Israel, during Blue Flag on November 27, 2013. On the vertical tail are the "LN" tail code of the 48th Fighter Wing and the blue tail band, with white edging, of the 492nd Fighter Squadron.

Two US Air Force F-15E Strike Eagles fly in formation over northern Iraq around dawn on September 23, 2014, after conducting airstrikes in Syria. These aircraft were part of a large coalition strike force that was the first to attack targets in Syria of the terror organization that called itself "the Islamic State in Iraq and the Levant" (ISIL), also called "Islamic State in Iraq and Syria" (ISIS) or referred to by the Arabic acronym "Daesh" or "Dâ'ish," derived from the group's Arabic name: ad-Dawlah al-Islâmîyah fî al-'Irâq wa-ash-Shâm.

A F-15C of the 144th Fighter Wing from Fresno, California, prepares to depart from the Canadian Forces Base Goose Bay in Labrador, Canada, on a mission on October 22, 2015, during Vigilant Shield 16. The exercise was held in Newfoundland and Labrador.

Speed brake deployed, an F-15E with the 428th Fighter Squadron lands at Luke Air Force Base, Arizona, on November 19, 2015, during the training exercise Forging Sabre, a joint exercise with Republic of Singapore armed forces. Singapore and US flags are painted on the tail for the occasion. *Senior Airman James Hensley / US Air Force*

F-15E, serial number 98-0134, of the 492nd Fighter Squadron, 48th Fighter Wing, prepares to depart RAF Lakenheath to support Operation Inherent Resolve on November 12, 2015. The wing was deploying six F-15Es to Incirlik Air Base, Turkey, to conduct counter-ISIL missions.

The pilot and the WSO of an F-15E Strike Eagle of the 48th Fighter Wing wait expectantly for clearance to take off from RAF Lakenheath, bound for Incirlik Air Base, to support Operation Inherent Resolve, November 12, 2015.

An F-15E Strike Eagle of the 48th Fighter Wing (the "Statue of Liberty Wing") lands at Incirlik Air Base, Turkey, on November 12, 2015. Among the underwing stores are AIM-120 AMRAAMs and two travel pods. (Note: The two travel pods are mounted on the CFTs, although it does appear that the rear one is mounted below the right drop tank.)

A crewman from the 494th Fighter Squadron exits from his F-15 while the other crewman stands on the fuselage, upon arriving at Incirlik Air Base on November 12, 2015. The insignia of the 494th Fighter Squadron is on the front of the CFT.

As darkness approaches, a column of three F-15Es taxis behind a follow-me car after landing at Incirlik Air Base on November 12, 2015. Soon, these Strike Eagles would be flying all-weather strike missions against ISIL forces both in Iraq and Syria.

Boeing F-15E-62-MC Strike Eagle, serial number 98-0131, with the 48th Fighter Wing, is preparing for takeoff from RAF Lakenheath, bound for Incirlik Air Base, Turkey, from where it will conduct missions against ISIL in Iraq and Syria under Operation Inherent Resolve, on November 12, 2015. *Senior Airman Erin Trower / USAF*

F-15C-38-MC, serial number 84-0017, assigned to the 144th Fighter Wing, prepares for takeoff at the Fresno Air National Guard Base on January 22, 2016. This plane was part of eight F-15s bound for Nellis Air Force Base to participate in the Red Flag 16-01 exercise.

After a crack was discovered in the wing of F-15C-21-MC, serial number 78-0482, assigned to the 142nd Fighter Wing, Portland, Oregon, the Depot Field Team from the 402nd Aircraft Maintenance Group, Robins Air Force Base, Georgia, is removing the old wings on December 6, 2016, preparatory to installing new ones.

In a companion view to the preceding photo, the Depot Field Team, 402nd Aircraft Maintenance Group, has separated the left wing from the fuselage of the F-15C. With the wing removed, details of the interior of the wing-root area are available, including plumbing and the wing-attachment lugs.

The setting sun, light poles, and security fences provide the backdrop for an F-15E Strike Eagle of the 48th Fighter Wing as it taxis the runway at Incirlik Air Base, Turkey, on November 12, 2015. The deployment was in coordination with the Turkish government.

F-15C-23-MC, serial number 78-0538, of the 144th Fighter Wing taxis at Nellis Air Force Base after landing on February 2, 2016, as part of Red Flag 16-1, a realistic combat-training exercise involving air, space, and cyber forces of the United States and its allies.

F-15E-49-MC, serial number 90-0238, of the 366th Fighter Wing flies over Iraq on March 17, 2016, on a mission against ISIL fighters. On the vertical tails are the orange bands with black tiger stripes that pertain to the 391st Fighter Squadron, and the squadron insignia is on the CFT.

A 67th Fighter Squadron F-15C returns to Kadena Air Base, Japan, after a flight on July 29, 2016. This plane had logged 10,000 flight hours, making it the first F-15 based at Kadena to achieve that distinction. The 18th Fighter Wing's "ZZ" code is on the tail.

A Massachusetts Air National Guard F-15C of the 104th Fighter Wing comes in for a landing at Graf Ignatievo, Bulgaria, on September 8, 2016. It was part of a force of four F-15Cs sent to assist the Bulgarian air force to police the host nation's sovereign airspace.

An US Air Force F-15E Strike Eagle from the 48th Fighter Wing at RAF Lakenheath lands on November 12, 2015, at Incirlik Air Base, Turkey. Six F-15Es had been deployed in support of Operation Inherent Resolve and counter-ISIL missions in Iraq and Syria. As an air-to-air and air-to-ground fighter aircraft, the F-15E specializes in gaining and maintaining air superiority, and few adversaries can match it in either role.

On August 24, 2016, F-15C-35-MC, serial number 83-0012, of the 122nd Fighter Squadron, 159th Fighter Wing, prepares for takeoff at Nellis Air Force Base during Red Flag 16-4. These were practice exercises to accustom crews to highly contested combat environments.

An F-15C assigned to the 194th Expeditionary Fighter Squadron, California Air National Guard, buzzes the flight line during an air show at Campia Turzii, Romania, on July 23, 2016, during the squadron's six-month deployment to Europe in support of NATO.

An Israeli F-15I, exhibiting serial number 223 and assigned to the 69th "Hammers" Squadron, takes off from Uvda Air Base on a mission during Exercise Juniper Falcon on May 7, 2017. The dome to the rear of the cockpit canopy houses high-bandwidth satellite-communications equipment.

F-15E-46-MC, serial number 88-1707, flies over Iraq on November 29, 2016, carrying a mixed load of JDAMs, GBUs, and air-to-air missiles in the war against ISIL. This plane is assigned to the 366th Operations Group, based at Mountain Home Air Force Base, Idaho.

A MiG-29 Fulcrum of the Bulgarian air force is in the foreground, and several F-15C Eagles are in the background, in a photo taken during a visit by the 122nd Expeditionary Fighter Squadron to Graf Ignatievo Air Base, Bulgaria, in support of Operation Atlantic Resolve in late April 2017.

The right engine has been removed from an F-15C during Exercise Northern Edge 17 at Joint Base Elmendorf-Richardson in Alaska on May 4, 2017. The engine, which was burning excessive oil, was pulled from the plane and replaced with another engine in under three hours.

An airman from the 48th Component Maintenance Squadron uses a penlight to inspect a Pratt & Whitney F100-PW-229 engine in a shop at Royal Air Force Lakenheath, England, on December 12, 2017. The engine is from an F-15E of the 48th Fighter Wing.

McDonnell Douglas F-15E-51-MC Strike Eagle, serial number 91-316, from the 492nd Expeditionary Fighter Squadron is being prepared for takeoff next to a hardened hangar at a base in Southwest Asia on October 9, 2017. In the background, an F-16 Falcon is taking off on a mission.

Personnel from the 173rd Fighter Wing and 550th Fighter Squadron and their families greet Santa Claus as he disembarks from an F-15D during the wing's annual children's Christmas party at Kingsley Field, Oregon, on December 3, 2017.

The aircrew of McDonnell Douglas F-15E-61-MC Strike Eagle, serial number 97-0219, from the 492nd Fighter Squadron, 48th Fighter Wing, are performing their preflight inspection at RAF Lakenheath, England, on February 6, 2019. The plane is in a "heritage" camouflage and markings scheme in emulation of the Republic P-47 Thunderbolt fighter-bombers the 492nd Fighter Squadron flew in Europe in World War II. Under the fuselage are a LANTIRN pod (partially hidden by the boarding ladder) and a Lockheed Martin Sniper advanced targeting pod. On the wing pylon launchers are an AIM-9 Sidewinder and an AIM-120 AMRAAM without the fins installed.

An F-15E from the 493rd Fighter Squadron departs from its base at RAF Lakenheath, England, on February 6, 2019. This aircraft too is wearing the heritage camouflage and markings scheme, which had been publicly unveiled during a ceremony a week earlier, on January 31. These heritage markings included the red-and-white checkerboard section, red rudders, and the black-and-white invasion stripes that the squadron's Thunderbolts wore during and following the 1944 Normandy invasion.

An Israeli air force F-15A, serial number 667, takes off from Uvda Air Base during Blue Flag 2019, on November 5, 2019. On the right vertical tail is a stencil of an eagle about to pounce on a target, while on the inboard side of the left vertical tail is a cartoonish depiction of an eagle's head.

The landing gear is being retracted on an F-15E Strike Eagle from the 492nd Fighter Squadron as it takes off from RAF Lakenheath, England, for a routine training flight on November 3, 2020. On pylons under the engine-air intakes are a LANTIRN pod (*right side*) and a Lockheed Martin Sniper advanced targeting pod.

F-15C-29-MC, serial number 80-0053, an Eagle from the 85th Test and Evaluation Squadron, 53rd Wing, takes part in an aerial-refueling operation above Northern California on May 14, 2021. On the vertical fin is a marking for "ANG AFRC TEST CENTER" (Air National Guard Air Force Reserve Command Test Center, based in Tucson, Arizona), and in the shadows toward the front of the main fuselage is the insignia of that test center. On the pylon launchers are inert AIM-120 AMRAAM air-to-air missiles. Inscribed below the windscreen is "LT COL WES 'ROCC' TURNER."

The colorfully painted and marked Eagle is F-15C-23-MC, serial number 78-0543 and manufacturer's serial number 0534/C076, at Kingsley Field, Klamath Falls, Oregon, on March 1, 2022. Nicknamed "SANDMAN" and attached to the 173rd Fighter Wing, this Eagle made its debut in these markings in January 2020. On the inside of both vertical tails is artwork in memory of the namesake of Kingsley Field, 2Lt. David R. Kingsley, a B-17 Flying Fortress bombardier who was posthumously awarded the Congressional Medal of Honor for saving the life of a fellow crewman, at the expense of his own, during a raid on Ploesti, Romania.

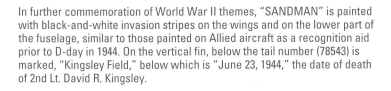

In further commemoration of World War II themes, "SANDMAN" is painted with black-and-white invasion stripes on the wings and on the lower part of the fuselage, similar to those painted on Allied aircraft as a recognition aid prior to D-day in 1944. On the vertical fin, below the tail number (78543) is marked, "Kingsley Field," below which is "June 23, 1944," the date of death of 2nd Lt. David R. Kingsley.

"SANDMAN" is viewed from the right rear as the pilot prepares to take off on a training mission. Part of the portrait of Lt. Kingsley on the inside of the left vertical tail is visible. To the front of the cockpit, the "SANDMAN" inscription, black-and-orange checkerboard pattern, and three gray bombs are present, as on the right side of the fuselage.

First flown in 1972, the McDonnell Douglas (later Boeing) F-15 Eagle was conceived as an absolute air-superiority fighter, drawing on lessons learned in Vietnam. While within the USAF the aircraft has recently been eclipsed in the air superiority role by the F-22, the F-15E variant continues to serve admirably in the strike role. This F-15E Strike Eagle from the 391st Expeditionary Fighter Squadron at Bagram Air Base, Afghanistan, launches heat decoys during a close-air-support mission over Afghanistan.